Thinking Strategies
for Student
Achievement

SECOND EDITION

W9-ABZ-608

Thinking Strategies

for Student Achievement

**IMPROVING
LEARNING
ACROSS THE
CURRICULUM, K–12**

DENISE D. NESSEL
JOYCE M. GRAHAM

SECOND EDITION

CORWIN PRESS
A SAGE Publications Company
Thousand Oaks, California

For information:

Corwin Press
A Sage Publications Company
2455 Teller Road
Thousand Oaks, California 91320
www.corwinpress.com

Sage Publications Ltd.
1 Oliver's Yard
55 City Road
London EC1Y 1SP
United Kingdom

Sage Publications India Pvt. Ltd.
B-42, Panchsheel Enclave
Post Box 4109
New Delhi 110 017 India

Printed in the United States of America.

Library of Congress Cataloging-in-Publication Data

Nessel, Denise D., 1943-
Thinking strategies for student achievement : improving learning across the curriculum, K–12 / Denise D. Nessel, Joyce M. Graham.—2. ed.
    p. cm.
Includes bibliographical references and index.
ISBN 1-4129-3880-5 or 9-7814-1293-8808 (cloth : alk. paper)—ISBN 1-4129-3881-3 or 9-7814-1293-8815 (pbk. : alk. paper)
    1. Thought and thinking—Study and teaching. 2. Cognitive learning.
3. Academic achievement. I. Baltas, Joyce Graham. II. Title.
LB1590.3.N47 2007
370.15'23—dc22

2006006770

This book is printed on acid-free paper.

06 07 08 09 10 10 9 8 7 6 5 4 3 2 1

Acquisitions Editor:	Cathy Hernandez
Editorial Assistant:	Charline Wu
Production Editor:	Jenn Reese
Copy Editor:	Edward Meidenbauer
Typesetter:	C&M Digitals (P) Ltd.
Proofreader:	Caryne Brown
Indexer:	Judy Hunt
Cover Designer:	Rose Storey
Graphic Designer:	Lisa Miller

Contents

Preface

Our original purpose in writing this book was to provide K–12 classroom teachers with a collection of instructional strategies that develop students' thinking abilities while raising their academic achievement. We included research-based strategies that we ourselves had found effective with students and that teachers we knew had used successfully in their own classrooms. Readers liked the concise explanations of the strategies, the convenient organization of the book, and the practical, classroom-oriented examples.

In this second edition, we have kept to these same purposes while adding more strategies to the collection and including these additional features:

- more extensive explanations of the histories of the strategies and the principles of learning on which they are based
- references that readers can consult for more information about the strategies, including research that supports their use in the classroom
- more examples of how the strategies can be used at different grade levels and in different content areas, including examples in language arts, mathematics, science, and social studies
- sample lessons to illustrate how teachers have combined various strategies to increase the effectiveness of their instruction

The book's introduction gives overall perspectives on thinking and achievement in the classroom and establishes the context for the strategies we include in the book. We ordered the strategy chapters alphabetically for easy access and have organized the information in each chapter in this way:

Overview and Background. In this section, we give information about the purpose of the strategy, the pedagogical principles on which it is based, and its pedigree. In giving the background of the strategy, we provide a richer context for understanding its value and honor those whose efforts and thinking continue to be relevant to teaching and learning today. For these reasons, the references we cite include works from some years ago as well as recent writings.

Instructional Benefits. This section contains an at-a-glance listing of the primary advantages to students when the teacher uses the strategy in the classroom.

Step by Step. In this section is a step-by-step explanation of how to use the strategy. We include examples to clarify our explanations and suggestions to help make sure the use of the strategy proceeds smoothly.

Additional Suggestions. This section contains suggestions for using the strategy at different grade levels and in different content areas and for modifying the strategy to suit different circumstances.

The Resource section contains examples of actual lessons that illustrate how teachers have integrated different strategies effectively into a unit of instruction. All of these were taught by our colleagues who shared their successes with us. We hope these examples will encourage readers to design similar lessons for their own classrooms to improve all students' thinking and increase their achievement.

Acknowledgments

Corwin Press gratefully acknowledges the contributions of the following reviewers:

Patricia Allanson, Seventh Grade Mathematics Teacher
Deltona Middle School, Deltona, FL

W. Dorsey Hammond, Professor of Education
Salisbury University, Salisbury, MD

Karen Lukens, Second Grade Teacher
Hawthorne Elementary School, Sioux Falls, SD

Patty McGee, Fourth Grade Teacher
Norwood Elementary School, Norwood, NJ

Kael Sagheer, Fifth Grade Teacher
Willa Cather Elementary School, Omaha, NE

Anne Smith, Education Research Analyst, Office of Special
   Education Programs
U.S. Department of Education, Washington, DC

Jon Van Wagoner, Eighth Grade Reading Teacher
Eastmont Middle School, Sandy, UT

Leonard J. Villanueva, Sixth Grade Teacher
Honowai Elementary School, Waipahu, HI

Shawn White, Social Studies Teacher
Weston McEwen High School, Athena, OR

About the Authors

Denise D. Nessel, PhD, has diverse experience in education, having worked as a secondary English teacher, elementary reading specialist, reading clinician, university professor, district-level curriculum supervisor, codirector of a statewide staff-development project, curriculum manager at educational software companies, and consultant to schools around the country and abroad. She has conducted numerous workshops for teachers and administrators and has served as a consultant and writer for educational publishers and multimedia firms. She has written 12 books for teachers, several classroom resources, and a number of articles for professional journals. As a current associate of the National Urban Alliance for Effective Education (NUA), she focuses on teaching reading and writing as thinking processes in grades K–12.

Joyce M. Graham, PhD, is the Director of Professional Development for Scholastic RED, the professional development division of Scholastic, Inc. In this capacity, Dr. Graham is responsible for recruiting and training consultants as well as developing and managing Scholastic institutes and workshops. Before joining Scholastic, Joyce had her own educational consultant firm and worked with school districts across the country. Joyce was a classroom teacher for more than 15 years and brings her classroom experience to her work with teachers. Dr. Graham has coauthored several books for classroom teachers. She has also served as editor for several books focusing on professional development.

Introduction

Thinking: Levels, Purposes, and Contexts

Thinking skills are the most basic of all the skills that can be developed in the classroom and are the foundations of high achievement for all learners. Students learn to think effectively when they have many opportunities to think at different levels, for different purposes, and in different contexts as an integral part of their learning. From kindergarten through grade 12, they need daily challenges that develop, refine, and extend their thinking capacities while they acquire knowledge and build skills. This introduction elaborates on this viewpoint and provides a context for the instructional strategies presented in the chapters that follow: thinking strategies for student achievement. The context includes perspectives on thinking along with basic principles of learning that lead to engagement and high achievement.

Thinking at Different Levels

Cognitive psychologists and educators have consistently recognized that some kinds of thinking are of a higher order than others. For example, Vygotsky (1962, 1978) pointed out that we are born with the most basic cognitive functions but develop higher mental abilities, such as abstract reasoning, as we mature. He stressed that cognition is heavily influenced by the culture within which we are raised, the way we are socialized as we develop, and the different kinds of interactions we have with others. His emphasis on the importance of the sociocultural aspects of learning and cognition set the stage for a later interest in cooperative learning and other forms of student-to-student interaction that help to develop high-level thinking abilities in social contexts (Lyman, 1981; Kagan, 1994; Singham, 1998; Jensen, 1998, 2005).

Benjamin Bloom was another proponent of the concept of levels of thinking. He and his colleagues identified six levels and presented them in a taxonomy of educational objectives (i.e., cognitive actions in which students should engage; Bloom Englehart, Furst, Hill, & Krathwohl, 1956). Bloom's levels of thinking are listed here from lowest to highest in terms of complexity with examples of how each level of thinking might be manifested in action.

Bloom's Taxonomy of Educational Objectives (1956)

Level of Thinking	Examples of Actions
Knowledge	list, recognize, recall, define, repeat, memorize, label
Comprehension	explain, describe, categorize, restate, translate, infer, discuss
Application	illustrate, demonstrate, interpret, solve, use in a new context
Analysis	compare/contrast, examine, test, inquire, infer, diagram, differentiate, prioritize
Synthesis	design, construct, organize, formulate, integrate, predict, modify, formulate
Evaluation	judge, criticize, argue, defend, persuade, reframe, consider from a particular perspective

Later researchers revised the taxonomy, as shown on the following page, to suit current educational needs (Anderson et al., 2001). The reversal of the last two original levels reflects a belief that the creative thinking involved in synthesizing information and generating something new is at a higher level of complexity than is the critical thinking involved in critiquing and evaluating.

Jerome Bruner (1960) also suggested that learning involves at least three levels of cognitive activity: acquisition, transformation, and evaluation. From his perspective, effective learners assimilate information by reading, listening, viewing, or a combination of inputs. Then they work with the information, analyzing, connecting, applying, and in other ways putting it to some relevant use that

Bloom's Taxonomy of Educational Objectives Revised (2001)

Level of Thinking	Examples of Actions
Remembering	recall, recognize, identify
Understanding	explain, summarize, infer, categorize, compare
Applying	implement, execute, solve, demonstrate, use in novel context
Analyzing	detect patterns, understand relationships, organize into a structure
Evaluating	use criteria or standards to judge, critique, assess, consider from another perspective
Creating	generate, invent, produce, reorganize into new system

extends beyond mere acquisition. Finally, they evaluate the extent to which their transformations have resulted in correct analyses, connections, and applications. Bruner also stressed the importance of intuitive thinking as an adjunct to analytical thinking, both of which he presented as examples of higher-level cognition.

The framework known as Dimensions of Learning (DOL) also makes use of the concept of levels of thinking (Marzano et al., 1992). Dimensions 2, 3, and 4 represent increasingly higher levels of thought, whereas affective elements are contained in Dimension 1 and mental habits in Dimension 5. On the following page is the DOL framework with selected examples of how each dimension might be represented in action.

For many years, teachers have used the concept of levels of thinking in deciding on questions, prompts, and assignments to enhance students' thinking and learning. For example, the DOL framework was introduced with many specific suggestions for classroom applications (Marzano et al., 1992), and Pohl (2000) suggests ways in which Bloom's taxonomy can be used to plan engaging classroom activities with a focus on high-level thinking. Jensen (1998, 2005) stresses that cognitive challenge is a critical feature of instruction that helps students function successfully as thinkers and learners.

Other psychologists and educators have concentrated on analyzing different aspects of high-level thinking. For example, Williams (1970, 1993) investigated the interaction between cognitive and affective responses to information and experience. The high-level cognitive

Dimensions of Learning

Dimension	Examples of Actions
Positive Attitudes and Perceptions About Learning	think positively, feel accepted, be confident, feel willing and able to learn
Acquiring and Integrating Knowledge	use prior knowledge, represent learning in various ways, organize new learning for comprehension and retention
Extending and Refining Knowledge	comparing, classifying, engaging in inductive and deductive thinking, analyzing perspectives, abstracting
Using Knowledge Meaningfully	making decisions, investigating, solving problems, inventing
Productive Habits of Mind	seeking clarity, being open-minded, engaging in metacognition, persisting

elements he considers important are fluent thinking, flexible thinking, original thinking, and elaborative thinking, whereas the affective elements are risk taking, complexity, curiosity, imagination. Buzan and Buzan (1993) suggest how to increase one's thinking capacity by making deliberate use of associations and connections to think in new and "radiant" ways by constructing, refining, and extending meanings with Mind Maps. Robinson (1993) advises learners to approach new information with the intention of mastering it, not just memorizing it and forgetting it soon after. He suggests a number of strategies that keep learners actively involved in high-level thinking, for example, detecting the big picture, making predictions, raising substantive questions, determining the relative importance of information, and connecting new information to previous learning. Hyerle (2000) advocates the use of Thinking Maps, and other visual tools, to represent, organize, and facilitate such higher-level thought as comparing and contrasting, analyzing cause-effect relationships, and generating analogies. Paul (1995) and Paul and Elder (2005) focus on critical thinking, stressing behaviors such as questioning, generating and evaluating conclusions, remaining open-minded, and communicating effectively with others, echoing the work of earlier educators, such as Kelley (1947) and Postman and Weingertner (1969), who also stressed that critical thinking in the classroom is essential to preparing students adequately for life. Moses and Cobb (2001) argue that high-level thinking, especially in mathematics, is as important to the establishment of a just and egalitarian society as was the civil rights movement of the 1960s.

Students who do well in school are readily given opportunities to engage in high-level thought, the assumption being that they have acquired "the basics" and can now engage in critical and creative thinking. In contrast, students who have been less successful are ordinarily given simplified courses of study in which the emphasis is on the lowest levels of cognition, the assumption being either that they are not ready for high-level thinking or that they are not capable of it. However, considerable evidence exists that underachieving students benefit from and respond positively to more challenging tasks that require higher levels of thinking. Rose (1989) describes how easily students with a history of failure can begin to think of themselves as incapable of academic success but also how, with the right kind of support, they can perform at the highest levels. Cooper (2004) and Jackson (2005) confirm this perspective, synthesizing the research on underachievement and drawing on their own successful experience with students of color in urban schools. Knapp (1995) reports on the demonstrated value of meaning-based instructional approaches that engage students in high-level thinking, while Pogrow (1990, 2000) argues that explicit instruction in higher-order thinking skills is essential as students move from the primary grades into the intermediate grades, especially for those who are faltering academically. Nystrand and colleagues (Nystrand, Gamoran, Kachur, & Prendergast, 1997), Allington (2001), and Moses and Cobb (2001) make the same argument for adolescents, demonstrating that when secondary school teachers concentrate on high-level thinking, students respond by elevating the quality and quantity of their thought. Smith and Wilhelm (2002) report that adolescent males with a history of underachievement readily engage in high-level thinking and literate behavior outside of school even while they respond with indifference to most classroom activities. These researchers suggest that the right kinds of modifications to the boys' instructional programs enable them to demonstrate their true potential in school as well as outside of it. Mahiri (1998, 2004) stresses the value of redefining the concepts of literacy and instruction so as to make classroom learning both more cognitively challenging and more interesting and relevant to secondary students. Position papers from major professional organizations make the same points about adolescent learning: the most effective instruction for all students avoids a heavy emphasis on basic skills instruction in favor of deliberate attention to a variety of high-level thinking activities (Moore, Bean, Birdyshaw, & Rycik, 1999; National Council of Teachers of English, 2004).

At any grade level, teachers invite high-level thinking when they encourage students to bring their own perspectives to a lesson by asking questions such as *What do you think?* and *Why do you think so?* They engage high-level thinking when they devise ways of challenging students to tackle more complex, unfamiliar material in ways that lead to success. They provide opportunities for high-level thinking when they ask students to represent their learning in a variety of creative forms. Effective teachers actively seek ways of making high-level thinking a regular part of their students' classroom work.

Thinking for Different Purposes

Besides thinking at different levels, students need to think for a variety of purposes to develop their cognitive capacities fully. To illustrate, here are representative classroom activities, each of which involves a different purpose for thinking:

Figure out an unknown word when reading

Identify the topic of an informational account

State the main idea and supporting details of an informational account

Determine the theme(s) of a fictional narrative or dramatic presentation

Recall information from heard, read, or viewed material

Develop a concept by identifying attributes, examples, and non-examples

Combine information from different sources to draw conclusions

Interpret the meanings of symbols

Detect patterns in sequences of pictures, words, or numbers

Use information to make predictions or form hypotheses

Perceive relationships (e.g., analogical, mathematical, cause-effect)

Organize information into time lines, charts, or other visual displays

Paraphrase information or an explanation

Categorize words, information, or ideas in various ways

Represent information in a new way (e.g., represent a narrative in music)

Summarize an account or a story

Compare and contrast two objects, places, people, or perspectives

Analyze a written or spoken presentation for bias

Distinguish between fact and opinion

Use a rubric to evaluate a response or product

Notice the way ideas are organized (e.g., chronological, categorical)

Visualize a scene or a process

Infer character traits in narrative or dramatic pieces

Critique a point of view or an opinion

Judge the quality of a presentation such as a story, a video, or a speech

Synthesize information from multiple sources into a coherent whole

Judge the expertise of an author or presenter

Brainstorm a wide range of responses

Generate fruitful questions to guide an inquiry

See the big picture into which specific information fits

Appraise the validity and completeness of a source of information

Organize a random array into an orderly arrangement

Use specifics to construct a generalization

Connect what is learned on one occasion to what was learned on another

Weigh various alternative actions in order to select the most appropriate

The stated purpose of the task may not clearly convey the level of thinking required. For example, a categorizing task can involve sorting concrete objects on the basis of such easily detected attributes as color or size, or it can involve a more sophisticated classification system in which more than one arrangement is possible. Similarly, comparing and contrasting, detecting analogies, or discerning cause–effect relationships are easier with simple, highly familiar material and more challenging with more complex, less familiar material. The key to increasing thinking capacity is to vary the purposes for thinking in ways that are appropriately challenging, given the age of the students, their familiarity with the topic, and their experience with the kind of thinking they are being asked to do.

By identifying and articulating the cognitive purpose of a classroom task as well as the content to be taught, teachers can help all students become familiar with and use a wide variety of thinking processes. By deliberately varying the cognitive purposes from day to day and unit to unit, teachers can continue to increase students' thinking capacities while making them more aware of the thinking of which they are capable.

Most high-level thinking activities can be accomplished by students working alone, but individual work is ordinarily not as desirable as collaborative work. Effective teachers through the years have found that students' thinking and achievement are elevated and improved when they talk and work together about what they are learning, pooling their knowledge and sharing their perspectives (Britton, 1970; Torbe & Medway, 1981; Applebee, 1996; Nystrand et al., 1997; Keene & Zimmerman, 1997; Singham, 1998; Langer, 2002).

Thinking in Different Contexts

Each unit of study or content area affords a different context within which purposes for thinking and levels of thinking can be varied. To illustrate, here are some examples of sequences of activities in different contexts that suggest how thinking can become the core of an instructional plan. In each example, students are engaged in different purposes for thinking as well as in thinking at different levels:

Language Arts

In reading and responding to a work of fiction, students might

- recall the sequence of events in the narrative
- infer information about the characters that was not stated explicitly
- connect events in the narrative to events in real life
- compare the story's characters and themes with those of other stories
- visualize a scene from the story and represent it in a drawing

- critically evaluate the quality of the narrative in light of established criteria for such stories
- transform the narrative into a play and act it out

In writing a persuasive essay, students might

- find and summarize information on the target issue
- judge the validity of the sources of information
- form an opinion on the basis of information and personal experience
- organize ideas into an outline or map in preparation for writing
- use a rubric to evaluate the first draft and plan revisions
- provide (receive) response and constructive criticism to (from) peers

Mathematics

In learning how to compute and work with the area of rectangles, students might

- recall the formula for computing the area of a rectangle
- apply the formula to compute the areas of a variety of rectangles in practice exercises
- compare several rectangles to determine which one has the largest area
- compute the area of various rectangular living spaces in the context of figuring out the least expensive way to cover the floors
- rank a set of rectangular spaces in terms of economy based on how costly they would be to decorate with a specific surface covering
- design a structure according to specifications (e.g., a five-room structure in which the floor area of each room is different but with a total area that does not exceed 1,200 square feet)

In developing understandings of measures of central tendency, students might

- collect information that yields a range of data points
- organize the data points from one extreme to the other
- analyze the data by computing the mean, median, and mode
- represent the mean, median, and mode graphically
- interpret the meanings of the analyzed data
- present the findings in a way that enables peers to understand the three measures of central tendency

Social Studies

In learning about an era in history, students might

- paraphrase information about the era they find in different sources
- compare and contrast two important people from the era
- represent the chronology of a complex sequence of events from the era in a time line
- analyze the causes and effects of a key event that occurred during the era
- consider the same historical event from several social or cultural perspectives that were relevant at the time of the event
- synthesize information about the era from several sources into a coherent whole

In learning the basics of democracy as a political system, students might

- restate the important elements of democracy as explained in a textbook
- compare a democratic political system with a dictatorship
- categorize various political activities as democratic or dictatorial
- debate the merits of a democracy and of a dictatorship
- analyze various current events in the context of the features of a democracy
- generate questions about aspects of democracy to guide further learning

Science

In learning about a specific animal, such as an octopus, students might

- observe an octopus firsthand and represent observations in drawing
- form hypotheses about octopus behavior based on firsthand observations
- gather factual information about the octopus to check hypotheses
- compare the octopus with other sea creatures
- synthesize information in a multimedia presentation about the octopus
- take and defend a position on the importance of the octopus to the ecology of the sea

In learning information related to a system of the human body (e.g., the respiratory system), students might:

- summarize information about the respiratory system in their own words
- define and explain key terms associated with the respiratory system
- collect and analyze information that will help them understand the functioning of their own respiratory systems
- represent the functioning of the respiratory system visually and verbally (e.g., in a labeled picture or diagram)
- compare and contrast the newly learned system with a previously learned system (e.g., compare the respiratory system with the circulatory system)
- create a presentation that effectively argues for a specific regimen of eating and physical exercise that would be most beneficial for maintaining the effectiveness of the respiratory system

In each example, although the content is the primary focus of the learning activities, thinking is a vital element before, during, and after learning. Students are not simply taking information in but are organizing, discussing, questioning, analyzing, representing, synthesizing, interpreting, evaluating, and in other ways processing and responding to that information. They are using it in ways that lead to comprehension, retention, and intelligent use of the material.

Conclusion

Teachers can help all students be successful by using instructional strategies that lead them to think at high levels for different purposes in different contexts. The chapters that follow contain thirty such strategies that can be used across grade levels and content areas. All have been used by classroom teachers in a wide variety of schools, including schools with high percentages of underachieving students; many have been in use for decades. These strategies are powerful because they reflect important principles of learning. Effective teachers understand these principles:

- Students must bring their own perspectives to lessons so that they will see the relevance of the content to their own lives.
- Students must make thoughtful and active use of their prior knowledge in order to learn new information.

- Students need challenges to keep them motivated and engaged in learning.
- Students need opportunities to talk to each other to construct, process, and reflect on meanings while hearing and appreciating one another's points of view.
- Students need to represent their learning in interesting and creative ways that enhance their comprehension and retention.

When teachers honor these principles by using strategies such as those presented here, they will help all students think and achieve at high levels and also derive genuine satisfaction from their experiences as learners.

1

Analogies

Overview and Background

An analogy is a way of stating a comparative relationship between two sets of terms. A and B (of the first set) are related to each other in the same way that C and D (of the second set) are related to each other. An analogy is often represented as follows: A : B :: C : D. For example, the governor is the elected head of a state in the same way that the mayor is the elected head of a city. This comparison can be represented in this analogy: governor : state :: mayor : city.

When one set of words is more familiar than the other, the meaning of the unfamiliar is illuminated by what is known about the familiar. For example, when students are learning about the functioning of the human heart, they can be taught that the heart moves blood through the body somewhat as a water pump moves water from a reservoir: heart : blood :: pump : water.

Incomplete analogies are often included in standardized tests because completing them correctly is considered evidence of high-level thinking. Studying and creating analogies helps students develop comprehension of vocabulary and concepts as they improve their reasoning ability and their critical thinking skills. Understanding analogies can be challenging for students because the nature of the relationship may not be immediately obvious. For this reason, it's important for teacher and students to state the nature of the relationship explicitly when discussing an analogy. Also, the convention of single and double colons can be difficult for some students to grasp, so using a different format, such as a Bridge Map, can help students more easily understand this kind of comparison (Hyerle, 1996, 2000).

Analogies are useful in subject areas to enhance learning of key concepts. For example, the concept of inverse operations in mathematics can be represented in an analogy (division : multiplication :: subtraction : addition), as can equivalence between fractions and decimals (1/2 : .50 :: 3/4 : .75). In an American History class, the roles of historical figures can be learned by means of analogy (Union Army : Ulysses S. Grant :: Confederate Army : Robert E. Lee).

For more information about using analogies in the classroom, see Huff-Benkoski and Greenwood (1995) and Venville and Dawson (2004).

Instructional Benefits of This Strategy

- develops understanding of the nature of various kinds of relationships
- helps students identify and analyze relationships
- develops and refines students' understanding of the specific vocabulary and concepts that are used in analogies
- develops critical thinking abilities in students

Step by Step

These suggested steps for teaching analogies are best done in the sequence given here. The steps may take several days or more to complete.

1. Give students examples of pairs of words that are related or associated in various ways, for example:

day	night
mother	child
wheel	bicycle
frosting	cake
acorn	oak

2. Have students state the relationship between the items in each pair. For example, the relationships for the pairs in Step 1 are:

day/night	Day is the opposite of night.
mother/child	A mother is a parent of the child.
wheel/bicycle	A wheel is part of a bicycle.
frosting/cake	Frosting is used to decorate a cake.
acorn/oak	An acorn grows into an oak.

3. Have students think of other pairs of words that are related in the same ways as the originals and list those alongside the pairs, being sure to order the words in the same way if order is relevant. For example:

day/night	up/down, cold/hot, front/back
mother/child	female dog/puppy, female cat/kitten
wheel/bicycle	leg/chair, eraser/pencil, bristle/brush
frosting/cake	whipped cream/sundae, embroidery/shirt
acorn/oak	child/adult, pumpkin seed/pumpkin

4. Model for students how to create the analogy using the conventions of a formal statement of analogy. Point out that the ordering of items on each side of the "equation" is important.

frosting : cake :: embroidery : shirt
(NOT frosting : cake :: shirt : embroidery)

wheel : bicycle :: leg : chair
(NOT wheel : bicycle :: chair : leg)

5. To reinforce the kind of thinking that's required for analogies, show students how to express the comparison in a sentence that clearly gives the nature of the relationship. For example:

frosting : cake :: embroidery : shirt

Frosting is used to decorate a cake just
as embroidery is used to decorate a shirt.

wheel : bicycle :: leg : chair

A wheel is part of a bicycle just as a leg is part of a chair.

6. Give students analogies with one term missing and have them work in pairs or groups to complete the analogy, write a sentence expressing the comparison, and write a sentence stating the nature of the relationship. For example:

convertible : car :: yacht : _____ (boat)

A convertible is a type of car just as a yacht is a type of boat.

Relationship: specific instance within a category

envelope : letter :: backpack : _____ (books or other items)

An envelope is a container for a letter just as a backpack is a container for books or other items.

Relationship: container and contents

7. When students understand how to complete analogies and write corresponding sentences, have them work in teams to generate new analogies to express comparisons within the curriculum content they are learning.

In teaching analogies, it can be useful to concentrate at first on common types of relationships until students become comfortable with the process of analogical thinking. Here are some relationships that form the basis of many analogies:

Nature of the Relationship	Sample Analogy
synonym	happy : joyous :: irritated : cranky
antonym	day : night :: in : out
worker and tool used	gardener : hoe :: carpenter : saw
tool and object it's used upon	hammer : nail :: scissors : cloth
function of a tool	safety pin : fasten :: pencil : write
creator and work created	writer : novel :: composer : symphony
part to whole	petal : flower :: pocket : jacket
masculine and feminine	actor : actress :: bull : cow
symbol and what it stands for	heart : love :: flag : nation
category and instance	cat : Persian :: automobile : convertible
cause and effect	germ : disease :: fertilizer : growth
effect and cause	tidal wave : earthquake :: mudslide : excessive rain

Additional Suggestions

- Have students work in teams to create analogies with information from a completed content-area unit. The teams can present their creations as incomplete analogies for the rest of the class to figure out. Have teams write out each of their analogies fully, along with the expression of the analogy in a sentence and a statement about the nature of the relationship. Check their work to make sure they have analogies that accurately express the target relationship. Then have teams present the first three terms, inviting the rest of the class to guess the fourth term and state the nature of the relationship.

- Analogies can also be used to assess students' knowledge. When designing a content-area test, include several incomplete analogies as test items. To be sure students understand the relationship, have them complete the analogy and explain the meaning in a sentence. Alternatively, you may want to use multiple-choice items. For example:

  find : found :: mind : _____

  minded, mind, mound, brain

  Nature of the relationship:

  Answer:

  find : found :: mind : *minded*

  Nature of the relationship: present and past tense of a verb

- Challenge students to generate analogies about the topics they are studying. These may involve types of relationships that are less common than the ones given in the table above. Here are some examples in mathematics:

  square : perimeter :: circle : circumference

  The term for the measured distance around a square is "perimeter" just as the term for the measured distance around a circle is "circumference."

  triangle : three :: pentagon : five

  A triangle has three sides just as a pentagon has five sides.

- Invite students to generate analogies based on their daily experiences. These may involve types of relationships that are less common than the ones given in the table above. Here are some examples:

    McDonald's : hamburger :: KFC : fried chicken

    The signature food of McDonald's is the hamburger just as the signature food of KFC is fried chicken.

    Harley-Davidson : motorcycles :: Nike : sportswear

    Harley-Davidson manufactures motorcycles just as Nike manufactures sportswear.

Most students will enjoy generating analogies about their favorite music and musical groups, actors and films, books and authors, sports and other leisure activities, food, and other such things relating to popular culture.

2

Anticipation Guide

Overview and Background

An anticipation guide is a set of statements based on material students are about to read, hear, or view. Students agree or disagree with the statements, discussing and debating their hypotheses and supporting their opinions with reasons from their own background of experience. Then they turn to the material to get more information. Finally, they consider the statements again, talk about how their thinking has changed, and review what they have learned. Ordinarily, anticipation guides are used with informational text, such as part of a chapter in a textbook or an article in a newspaper or magazine. The material might also be a video documentary, details presented on a Web site, a guest speaker's presentation, or some other source of information.

The anticipation guide was originally designed for use in secondary-school classrooms at a time when content-area teachers began focusing on helping students read informational materials more effectively. The strategy has also been used successfully for many years in elementary-school classrooms. Anticipation guides have remained popular across the grades with teachers of social studies, science, math, literature, and other subject areas who want to prepare students for learning new information while making their reading of expository material more purposeful and enjoyable as well as increasing their thinking abilities. For early discussions of the strategy as well as recent commentaries and applications, see the following selected readings: Herber (1978); Nelson-Herber (1985); Nessel, Jones, and Dixon (1989); Brozo and Simpson (1999); Cunningham, Hall, and Cunningham (2000); and Vacca and Vacca (2002).

Instructional Benefits of This Strategy

- activates prior knowledge
- sharpens critical listening and thinking skills
- arouses curiosity, increasing motivation to read
- generates specific purposes for reading
- promotes active involvement in reading
- creates a pleasurable sense of discovery when finding information related to the hypotheses
- enhances retention by making information memorable

Step by Step

Before being successful with anticipation guides, students need experience speculating, listening to and responding directly to one another, and debating different points of view. When they are comfortable with these aspects of the process, here are the steps to follow:

1. Write several declarative statements about the topic that are based on information in the learning material. Some of the statements should be true and some should be false, but all should be worded so that they sound plausible and will probably bring about differences of opinion among students. The examples that follow illustrate the possibilities across subject areas:

   Here is an anticipation guide that was designed for use in a second-grade science lesson:

Snails

Read these sentences about snails. Do you agree or disagree?

_____ 1. Baby snails come from eggs.

_____ 2. Snails eat insects.

_____ 3. Snails eat plants.

_____ 4. A snail's eyes are at the ends of its feelers.

_____ 5. Snails can crawl over sharp things without being hurt.

Here is an anticipation guide that was designed for use in a fourth-grade science lesson:

Birds' Nests

Directions: Read these sentences about birds' nests. Do you agree or disagree? Put *A* (Agree) or *D* (Disagree) to show what you think.

_____ 1. Birds use grass to build their nests.

_____ 2. Some birds use other birds' nests.

_____ 3. Male and female birds build nests together.

_____ 4. If the eggs get cold, they will not hatch.

_____ 5. Mother birds sit on their nests all day.

Here is an anticipation guide designed for use in a middle-school math lesson:

Triangles

Directions: Here are some statements about triangles. Decide if you Agree (A) or Disagree (D) with each, and write *A* or *D* on the line to show your thinking. Be prepared to explain your reasoning.

_____ 1. All triangles have the same number of angles and sides.

_____ 2. When you add up the angles in a triangle, you always get the same number.

_____ 3. *Congruent* triangles have the same shape but are different sizes.

_____ 4. A triangle that has three sides of different lengths is called a *scalene* triangle.

_____ 5. A triangle is the same as a polygon.

Here is an anticipation guide that was designed for use in a high-school history lesson:

Early Chicago

Directions: Here are some statements about Chicago in the 19th century. Put an *A* or *D* in front of each to show if you Agree or Disagree with it. Be prepared to explain your reasoning and defend your point of view.

_____ 1. Chicago had about 50,000 settlers in 1835.

_____ 2. Muddy streets were a major problem in Chicago in 1850.

_____ 3. The city's early growth was related to the Erie Canal.

_____ 4. The first permanent theater was established in 1837.

_____ 5. Early Chicago had the best opportunity for young people of any city of its time.

2. Before students read (listen, view), have them work with partners or in small groups to discuss the items and decide on their responses and their reasoning, then share their thinking with the whole class. The particular approach to responding can vary. For example, in the primary grades, put the statements on a large chart, read them aloud one by one, and have students talk briefly with a partner about the item before discussing it as a whole class. In the upper-elementary grades, organize students into small groups, give each group a copy of the guide, and have a recorder write the responses decided on by the group. Then have groups convene as a whole class to share their thoughts. At the secondary level, give the students a copy of the guide and have them mark their answers

individually, then compare notes in small groups in preparation for the groups debating their responses as a whole class.

3. In leading the discussion, frequently ask "Why do you think so?" and "Do you all agree?" to encourage students to explain their reasoning, make good use of their existing knowledge, and debate one another. For example, if students agree that some birds use other birds' nests, ask them why birds might do that and if they think all birds use other birds' nests or only some do. If students say they think the Erie Canal was related to the growth of Chicago, ask them when and where they think the Erie Canal was built, who might have used it, and in what way that use might have been connected with early Chicago. By pressing students (gently and with good humor) to search for connections, think more deeply, draw tentative conclusions, and debate their ideas, even when they're not sure they're right, you'll help them develop an inquiring habit of mind and will raise their curiosity while increasing the depth of their thinking. Also, you'll encourage them to lay the foundations for assimilating the new information. Be sure not to let students know who's right (if anyone is) so that they'll keep thinking and talking about the statements and will not be focused solely on the correct answer.

While encouraging students to use what they know to defend their hypotheses, you will also have a chance to achieve a better understanding of your students' backgrounds and perspectives and encourage them to appreciate each other's knowledge and experience. When students are expected to explain their reasoning, they rather naturally draw on what they know, what they have heard from others, or what they have read or seen on television. Sharing perspectives deepens the connections between participants in the discussion and strengthens their understanding of each other.

4. Have students read the material to confirm or revise their ideas. Then have them return to the guide and discuss the statements again in light of what they've learned. Encourage them to cite evidence from the material to support their revisions.

Because an anticipation guide is used as an introduction to a body of material or a unit of instruction, you'll need to spend more time discussing important points, developing key concepts, and having students reread the material for other purposes. In bringing the anticipation-guide lesson to a close, however, you may want to ask one or more wrap-up questions like these:

What was the most interesting thing you learned?

What was the most surprising thing you learned?

How would you summarize what you learned?

What questions do you have at this point?

Additional Suggestions

- If your students are not familiar with anticipation guides, they may need several experiences with them before they begin to respond effectively and enthusiastically. They may also need extra reassurance that the quality of their thinking is more important before reading than the extent and accuracy of their existing knowledge.

- At first, you may be concerned about presenting students with false statements or allowing them to verbalize misconceptions, thinking that they'll remember those rather than the correct information. However, students soon learn that anticipation-guide statements, and anything said in the pre-reading discussion, may be true or false and that they can't be sure until they get more information. Learning to take this perspective helps them to develop critical reading skills. To insure retention of correct information you may want to have students revise the statements after they read so that they are all correct.

- Writing statements for an anticipation guide is an art. When you write one, think about how your students might respond. If you can think of plausible reasons to agree and to disagree with the statement, then the correct answer will probably not be obvious to the students. Also, each time you design an anticipation guide, observe how the students respond. Which statements provoked lively debate? Which ones didn't generate much discussion? Use your observations to inform the design of the next one.

- Different kinds of items can be effective on anticipation guides. For some lessons, you may want to use factual statements that sound like true-false items, such as "Chicago had about 50,000 settlers in 1835." For other lessons, you may want to use statements of opinion, such as "Early Chicago had the best opportunity for young people of any city of its time." Whether you use factual statements, statements of opinion, or a combination will depend on the contents of the instructional material and what you consider most important in that material, given your goals.

3

Carousel
Brainstorming

Overview and Background

Carousal Brainstorming (Kagan, 1994) is a cooperative group activity developed years ago to engage the entire class in generating ideas. Students work in teams to brainstorm ideas at a home station, writing them on a large sheet of paper. Then the teams move from station to station, adding their ideas to those of the other groups. When the teams return to their home station, they read the ideas that have been added to their paper, raise questions about that new information, and add ideas they may have obtained from other groups. This strategy incorporates reading, writing, speaking, and listening in a natural, fluid way. It can be done before beginning a new unit of study to activate students' prior knowledge and set purposes for learning. It can also be used after a lesson or unit to review and restate information.

In a review of research on cooperative learning, Johnson, Johnson, and Holubec (1998) found that students who participated in cooperative learning activities such as Carousel Brainstorming had improved academic achievement, behavior, self-confidence, motivation, and attendance.

Instructional Benefits of This Strategy

- encourages students to think about what they know and express it in their own words
- reinforces learning by having students restate ideas orally and in writing
- gives students opportunities to listen to and read each other's ideas
- leads students to generate questions about what they have learned

Step by Step

Students may need some practice with Carousel Brainstorming before they can move smoothly from station to station and make good contributions to their own notes and the notes of others. The process will work best if the groups are small (2–4) and if each group member has a specific responsibility: for example, one student keeps the group on task, another writes the ideas, another speaks for the group when it is time to share, another offers positive comments and encouragement as the team works.

1. Decide on a topic or question to set the brainstorming in motion. The purpose of the brainstorming can be to prime students for information they are going to learn or review information from a completed unit. For example, if the unit is on the Revolutionary War, these topics would be appropriate: Declaration of Independence, Stamp Act, Colonies, and Ride of Paul Revere.

2. Organize the class into several teams and establish a home base for each team. Home bases should be positioned so that students can move easily from one to the other and so that enough space is left around each base for teams to gather and write. Interaction and movement may be easier if students stand during the whole activity.

3. Give each team a large sheet of chart paper or hang the paper on the wall near each home base. Provide each team with a marker of a unique color. (When each group writes in a unique color, the contributions of any given group can easily be identified.)

4. Assign or have students select their responsibilities (leader, writer, speaker, encourager). Have the writer write the topic

or question at the top of the chart paper. Teams can have the same topic, or each can have a different topic, perhaps subtopics within a unit. You may also want to give students a structure within which to write their ideas. For example, if they are brainstorming ideas in four different categories, have them divide the paper into four sections, one for each category of information.

5. Have each team brainstorm their ideas while the writer records the ideas on the chart paper. Writers should use sentences rather than single words or phrases to make sure the group's meaning is represented clearly. Allow at least five minutes.

6. Have the teams move in the same direction (e.g., clockwise) to the next station. When they get to their next station, they should:
   • Read what's already on the chart at that station.
   • Add new ideas, elaborate on ideas that are there, or write the same ideas in different words.
   • Represent the team's ideas in sketches if it is a challenge to write in words or if sketches would clarify meanings. (Drawing is an appropriate alternative for students who do not yet write easily.)

7. Have students rotate through all the stations, talking and reading and writing, until they return to their home base. At their home base, they should:
   • Read all the ideas on their chart.
   • Identify two to three statements they think are especially insightful or interesting to share with the whole class.
   • Generate one or two questions about new items they see on their charts.

   As students read and discuss the completed charts, discourage criticism about what "they" (other students) added to "our" (original) chart. Instead, encourage students to ask one another questions about the ideas that were added to their charts and suggest how questionable statements might be revised. This reflection and discussion should be an occasion for students to refine and extend their comprehension of the material while interacting productively with each other. Some classes may need guidance and practice to interact effectively.

8. Have team speakers present to the class the two or three interesting statements the group selected in step 7.

9. Have team speakers raise the questions their teams had about ideas added to their charts. Members of other teams may answer these questions. The color coding will allow easy identification of the team who wrote the information being questioned.

10. End the discussion with a team and class reflection of the group process as well as self-reflection for each individual regarding his or her effort and contribution.

Additional Suggestions

- Use Carousal Brainstorming as an end-of-unit activity in any content area. When teams have completed their charts and the class has finished sharing thoughts and discussing questions, have students write individual summaries of what they learned, using their team's chart as a source of ideas.

- Use Carousal Brainstorming as a follow-up to reading a novel or a biography with several important characters. Assign a different character to each team as the topic of their chart so that as teams rotate they write their ideas about a different character each time.

- Have students use the strategy as a prereading activity in a content-area unit and then add to the same charts after completing the unit. Have students group similar ideas from their chart and label each group to identify the major categories of information they learned about in the unit.

- Have students express final thoughts about what they have written on their charts, using any one of these techniques:

  Summarize the information in writing

  Provide reasons for their thinking

  Produce a drawing for each key concept

  Act out key concepts or events

  Report main ideas or common themes

4

Cloze Procedure

Overview and Background

The Cloze Procedure is a strategy for developing comprehension and inferential thinking skills. It makes use of a passage of text in which some words have been replaced with blanks. The reader writes in the words that have been deleted, inferring their identity by using the remaining words as clues. The activity gives students opportunities for inferential thinking and close reading. Readers who focus primarily on pronouncing words derive particular benefits because the strategy encourages them to construct meaning actively and gives them the experience of comprehension that Britton (1979) describes:

> We do not, as we read, add word meaning to word meaning—like watching coaches come out of a tunnel; rather it is like watching a photographic negative in a developing-dish, a shadowy outline that becomes etched in with more of the detail as we proceed. The finished picture represents a transformation, brought about by the text-as-we-have-interpreted-it—a transformation of our initial expectations. (p. 134)

The Cloze Procedure was devised more than 50 years ago as a way of measuring text readability. It was given its name because the objective is to close the gaps left in the passage by the deletions. To estimate the match between a reader and a text, the examiner gives the reader a passage with at least 50 blanks and computes the percentage of correct responses (correctly filled-in words). The criteria are as follows:

55% and above = independent level (The student can probably read and comprehend the material independently.)

38–54% = instructional level (The student can probably read and comprehend the material when guided by a teacher.)

37% and below = frustration level (The material is probably too difficult for the student even if the student's reading is guided by a teacher.)

Generations of teachers have used the Cloze Procedure to determine if their students can read curriculum materials. It is especially useful in secondary-school classrooms to estimate how difficult the curriculum materials might be for different students. Because the whole class can be tested at once, it is also an efficient way of making these estimations.

Soon after being introduced as a diagnostic technique, the Cloze Procedure was recognized as an effective instructional activity for building students' reading and thinking skills. Several modifications have been developed for specific instructional purposes and are described below. For early discussions of the strategy as well as recent commentaries and applications, including discussions about the kind of thinking involved in completing a cloze passage, see the following selected readings: Taylor (1953), Bormuth (1962), Goodman (1967), Bormuth (1968), Pikulski and Tobin (1982), and Carr and colleagues (1989).

Instructional Benefits of This Strategy

- activates linguistic knowledge
- refines inferential thinking abilities
- provides practice in the use of context clues to identify unfamiliar words
- develops the habit of careful, active reading

Step by Step

To be successful with the Cloze Procedure, students should be able to fill in the correct word or words orally when a speaker pauses before the end of an utterance. When students are first learning the strategy, the passage from which the cloze activity is created should be at a level that students can read comfortably on their own.

1. Select a text passage that students have not read before. An unfamiliar text is essential for stimulating inferential thinking. (If students are familiar with the text, they will be recalling the words rather than actively constructing meaning.) The passage can be of whatever length is appropriate for the students, though the maximum length ordinarily yields around 50 deleted words.

2. Copy the passage, leaving the first sentence intact. Starting with the second sentence, replace every nth word with a blank, using blanks of uniform length. Ordinarily, every fifth word is deleted, but n can be another number if desired. The higher the n (that is, the less frequent the deletions), the easier the activity. Double-space lines so that students will have room to write in their responses. Leave the last sentence intact. Here, as an example, is the beginning of a cloze passage in which every fifth word has been deleted:

> Once upon a time, a girl lived in a small cabin with her widowed father. Every day, the girl _____ her father worked in _____ garden, watering and weeding _____ fertilizing the vegetables that _____ their main source of _____. One day, as the _____ was harvesting beans from _____ vines that climbed a _____ at the far end _____ the garden, a curious _____ man stepped from the _____ and said, "Good morning, _____ dear! How are you this _____ day?"
>   The startled girl _____, "Who are you, sir?"
>   _____ little man jumped and _____ with glee. "I'm a _____!" he replied with a _____. "And I am here _____ help you."
>   "A wizard?" _____ the girl.
>   "Yes!" giggled _____ little man.

3. Make copies of the cloze passage for all the students and distribute them. Display the first sentence or two for the whole class to see. Demonstrate, by reading and thinking aloud, how to use the context to make inferences about the deleted words, pointing out specific syntactical and semantic clues if possible. For example, this is how you might think aloud to the class

about the first two blanks in the example, using "mmm" or a similar placeholder sound to represent the blank:

> Let me see if I can figure this out. The girl mmm her father worked. I'll bet that first missing word is "and." Let's see how that sounds. The girl *and* her father worked. That makes sense. I'll write in "and" for now and see if it still makes sense as I keep reading. The girl and her father worked in mmm garden. I can think of several words that make sense in that blank. In *a* garden, in *the* garden, in *their* garden. I'll try in *their* garden for now. I'm thinking that if they work in the garden every day, it probably belongs to them.

Tell students you might change your mind as you continue reading because words farther along in the passage may give you the clues you need to figure out words that have been deleted near the beginning. Explain that a cloze passage is something like a puzzle and that the challenge of figuring it out is interesting and fun.

4. Have students work in pairs or small groups to discuss their ideas as they fill in the rest of the blanks on their respective copies of the passage. Circulate to observe how they are doing and assure them that tentative responses are acceptable. Some students are reassured when they understand that even the most proficient readers are unable to fill in all the blanks correctly when they are working on a cloze passage. In fact, filling in only half of the blanks with the words that were deleted is considered a very good response.

5. When students have finished, have them share their thinking and explain their reasoning. Encourage debate.

6. Show students the intact passage so that they can check their guesses against the actual words. Here is the intact passage used as an example here.

> Once upon a time, a girl lived in a small cabin with her widowed father. Every day, the girl and her father worked in their garden, watering and weeding and fertilizing the vegetables that provided their main source of food. One day, as the girl was harvesting beans from the vines that climbed a trellis at the far end of the garden, a curious little man stepped from the bushes and said, "Good morning, my dear! How are you this fine day?"
>
> The startled girl replied, "Who are you, sir?"

The little man jumped and danced with glee. "I'm a wizard!" he replied with a giggle. "And I am here to help you."
"A wizard?" cried the girl.
"Yes!" giggled the little man.

7. Give students regular practice with a variety of cloze passages. Regular experience with cloze provides opportunities to discuss various linguistic clues to the deleted words while refining and extending inferential thinking skills. For ongoing practice, use either narrative passages or a combination of narrative and expository passages.

Additional Suggestions

- If students need practice using phonetic clues in conjunction with context clues while they are decoding text, give them the first letter or two of each deleted word as additional clues in a cloze passage. For example:

    Every day, the girl a_____ her father worked in th_____ garden, watering and weeding a_____ fertilizing the vegetables that p_____ their main source of f_____.

- If students need extra support as they are first learning the Cloze Procedure, give them a list of words from which to choose as they fill in the deleted words. This modification is especially useful for students whose native language is not English and thus who may not be able to think readily of the words they need.

- Because cloze passages from expository text can be more challenging, it's usually best to delete every seventh, eighth, or ninth word from these passages rather than every fifth word. With fewer deletions, more context is available from which inferences can be made about the missing words.

- To give students more than the usual context as a basis for their inferences, delete only selected words here and there. This variation is especially useful in content areas with texts that are dense with information or technical vocabulary. Completing the passage demands careful attention to meaning as well as inferential thinking, which, combined, ordinarily have a positive effect on comprehension of this kind of material. For example, a modified cloze passage from a mathematics text might look like this:

Two interesting facts about pine cones have to do with the arrangement of the segments of a cone. First, the _____ are arranged in spirals. Some of the _____ go in a clockwise direction, and the others ____ in an anticlockwise direction. Eight spirals go clockwise, and 13 ____ go anticlockwise. The second interesting _____ is that both ___ and ___ are Fibonacci numbers.

Here's the intact passage:

Two interesting facts about pine cones have to do with the arrangement of the segments of a cone. First, the segments are arranged in spirals. Some of the spirals go in a clockwise direction, and the others go in an anticlockwise direction. Eight spirals go clockwise, and 13 spirals go anticlockwise. The second interesting fact is that both 8 and 13 are Fibonacci numbers.

A modified cloze passage from a science text might look like this:

When people pay close attention to sharks, they appreciate how interesting and even amazing the creatures are. There are about 370 known shark species, and they are quite different from one another. The whale shark, the _____ of all, may reach a length of 60 feet, while a fully grown lemon _____ is much smaller. Some sharks, like the basking shark, ____ mainly krill or plankton, while others prey on larger fish. The angel shark blends into the background and waits for smaller _____ to swim by, while the cookie-cutter shark attacks aggressively by biting _____ out of its prey.

Here's the intact passage:

When people pay close attention to sharks, they appreciate how interesting and even amazing the creatures are. There are about 370 known shark species, and they are quite different from one another. The whale shark, the largest of all, may reach a length of 60 feet, while a fully grown lemon shark is much smaller. Some sharks, like the basking shark, eat mainly krill or plankton, while others prey on larger fish. The angel shark blends into the background and waits for smaller creatures to swim by, while the cookie-cutter shark attacks aggressively by biting pieces out of its prey.

- The Cloze Procedure provides a good base for discussions of word choice in conjunction with responding to literature or writing original compositions. To focus on word choice, delete all the instances of a particular part of speech from the passage, such as adjectives, adverbs, or verbs. Facilitate a discussion of the various words that might be appropriate in the blanks and the choices that would be best. For example, one part of the example passage might look like this:

  . . . a _____ man stepped from the bushes and said, "Good morning, my dear! How are you this _____ day?"

  Have students discuss which adjectives might be used to describe the man (odd, wizened, ugly, etc.) and the day (lovely, beautiful, promising, etc.), and which ones seem to be the best choices and why. Then have them work in pairs or small groups to complete the passage, inserting the adjectives they think are the best and sharing their decisions with the rest of the class.

- Sudoku puzzles are nonlinguistic analogues of the cloze procedure. They develop and refine the same kind of inferential thinking abilities and can be an interesting alternate way of engaging students in this important thinking process.

  An example of a Sudoku puzzle is shown below. The solver must put numerals in the blank cells so that each row, each column, and each 3×3 section contains every numeral from 1–9. Thus a numeral cannot be repeated in any row, column, or 3×3 section. Solving the puzzle requires inferring from the available clues (the provided numerals) where to put the numerals that have been deleted.

  For example, in the puzzle below, the shaded 3×3 box in the upper left-hand corner still needs the following numerals: 3, 5, 6, 8, and 9. Although it's not yet clear where those five numerals belong in that box, an inference can be made about where to place the 6. The location of a 6 in the third puzzle row from the top means that a 6 cannot be placed in any other cells in that row. And the location of a 6 in the column on the far left means that a 6 cannot be placed in any other cells in that column. Given these constraints, the only cell in which the 6 can be placed in the target 3×3 section is the open cell in the top row.

2		1						8
	4	7						
					6			5
6			1		2	3		7
					5	9		
	8						2	
			2		3			1

Sudoku puzzles appear in many daily newspapers and other periodicals and are also available at Sudoku Web sites, of which there are many. Two examples are www.sudoku.com and www.dailysu doku.co.uk

5

Cubing

Overview and Background

Cubing is a thinking activity that encourages students to explore meanings of a given object, concept, or phenomenon from six perspectives, each of which calls for a different kind of high-level thought. The stimulus is a cube that has six different prompts, one on each face: describe, compare/contrast, associate, analyze, apply, and argue for or against. Students respond to each of the six in turn, either orally or in writing.

Cubing has been used for many years as an engaging classroom activity, primarily in the upper elementary and secondary grades. It can be a quick warm-up discussion activity, a prewriting exercise, or the basis of a more extended composition. Ordinarily, the topic is a concrete object, although Cubing can be used to examine abstract ideas from the six different perspectives. For early discussions of the strategy as well as recent commentaries and applications, see the following selected readings: Cowan and Cowan (1980), Vaughan and Estes (1986), and Tomlinson (2001).

Instructional Benefits of This Strategy

- helps students think about a topic from multiple perspectives
- develops writing fluency

- develops flexibility in thinking
- encourages students to learn from each other by listening to each other's responses

Step by Step

Before being successful with Cubing, students need to understand each of the six modes of thinking that are used in Cubing. These are the important elements of each:

- To *describe* is to give attributes, details, or characteristics. For example, if the object is a crayon, writers might mention the crayon's color, the color and feel of the paper covering, the words and designs on the covering, the way the crayon feels when it's used as a writing implement, and the look of the resulting mark on the paper.
- To *compare/contrast* is to point out similarities and differences. For example, a crayon is similar to a pen in that one can write or draw on paper with it and different from a pen in that crayon marks can rub off, whereas ink ordinarily will not. A crayon might also be compared and contrasted with a pencil, a piece of chalk, a white-board marker, or another writing implement.
- To *associate* is to make connections. For example, a crayon might be associated with coloring books or drawing. A writer may also make idiosyncratic associations with a crayon, such as the memory of having received a box of crayons as a present.
- To *analyze* is to examine in order to explain structure and to note constituent parts and functions. For example, a crayon can be analyzed by noting that it is ordinarily made up of two parts: the hard, waxy stick that makes the marks and the paper cover that protects one's fingers.
- To *apply* is to indicate how something can be used. For example, a crayon can be used to create a drawing on paper or to color in a designated area such as is found in a coloring book. It might also be used to write a message or to mark a passage in a book or magazine. More unusual applications might include using it as an object in a collage or as a holiday ornament.

- To *argue for/against* is to enumerate advantages and disadvantages. For example, some advantages of a crayon are that it is inexpensive, colorful, and fun to use, while some disadvantages are that it may leave a stain on clothing, that it makes a relatively crude line, and that it is difficult to keep sharp.

You will probably want to explain and model each mode of thinking and have students practice each before combining them all in a cubing exercise. For students in the primary grades, you may want to combine only two or three modes at a time instead of all six. Here is a suggested sequence:

1. Decide how many groups of three or four you will have and prepare enough cubes so that each group will have one. Make cubes by folding sturdy paper into cubes or by repurposing wooden or plastic cubes. Label each face with one of the thinking processes: describe, analyze, compare and contrast, apply, associate, argue for or against.

2. Organize students into groups and give each group a cube. Announce the topic and tell students they will be exploring the topic from different perspectives, as shown on the faces of their cubes. Then have them turn their cubes so that DESCRIBE appears on top.

3. Tell students to focus on writing to describe the topic. Assure them that there's no "right" way to respond and that they should write whatever comes to mind to describe the topic. Have them all start at the same time and write for at least five minutes, or longer if you wish.

4. When the time is up, have students take turns reading what they wrote to the members of their group. By listening to each other, students will enhance their understanding of the topic and learn how the others in the group were thinking about it. This sharing also provides a short break before the next round of writing.

5. Now have students turn their cubes so that COMPARE/ CONTRAST appears on top and have them compare and contrast the topic with anything else they can think of. (You may want to give them a suggestion to make sure they have something in mind. For example, if the focus is a crayon, you might say "Compare and contrast a crayon with a pen.") When the

time is up, again have students read their writings aloud in their groups.

6. Continue this way until students have written in response to all six prompts on the cube, or fewer if you prefer.

7. For closure, lead a discussion with the whole class about how thinking about the topic in different ways affected their understanding of the topic and their writing. Here are some discussion prompts you may want to use:
   - Which kind of thinking was the easiest to do? Why?
   - Which kind of thinking did you enjoy the most? Why?
   - Which kind of thinking did you find the hardest? Why?
   - Which kind of thinking made you discover new aspects of the topic?
   - In what ways has your understanding of the topic improved?

Additional Suggestions

- Concrete objects or observable phenomena are usually much easier to use as cubing topics than abstract concepts. Students will be able to write most easily if they have the object or a picture of it in front of them or have recently experienced the phenomenon or event. Try a variety of topics to see which ones stimulate the best writing in your classroom. Here are a few ideas:

CONCRETE OBJECTS	PHENOMENA OR EVENTS
a book	a thunderstorm
a ruler	a breeze blowing in the trees
a fresh apple	lunchtime in the cafeteria
a backpack	a school ceremony
a water bottle	recess or the time between classes
a multiplication table	taking a test

- When students are familiar with the activity, let them determine the order of the perspectives they will use by having each group take a turn at tossing their cube to determine which perspective the class will use next.

- When students have completed cubing exercises in small groups several times, have them make their own individual cubes and do the same activity independently or with a partner.

- Encourage students to use Cubing to generate ideas before writing or to review information they've learned.

- Try Cubing in different content areas. In social studies, have students cube a famous person or an important moment in history, using one or more illustrations to spark ideas. In math, have students cube a bar graph, a ruler, or a calculator. In science, have students cube a flower, the human circulatory system, or something students can observe under a microscope. In English, have students cube a character from literature, or assign a different character to each small group.

- Cubing can be used as an oral exercise as well, with partners or small groups responding to each of the six prompts by talking with each other instead of writing and then sharing their thoughts with the class as a whole. Or students can take turns being the recorder for their small group, writing down what the others in the group say in response to each prompt.

6

Directed Reading-Thinking Activity (DRTA)

Overview and Background

A Directed Reading-Thinking Activity (DRTA) is a strategy for guiding readers through a text. They repeatedly speculate about what they will read next and then confirm or refute their hypotheses by reading. This approach develops critical thinking skills while also building vocabulary, comprehension, and reading fluency. The Directed Listening-Thinking Activity (DLTA) is a variation that involves the teacher reading the text aloud to the students. The questions used in a DRTA or DLTA vary somewhat, depending on whether the text has a narrative or expository structure.

Russell Stauffer designed the DRTA as an alternative to the Directed Reading Activity (DRA), a widely used method for guided reading. An important aspect of the DRA is stopping students periodically to ask them questions about the part they just read in order to monitor and develop their comprehension. The DRTA introduced a significant difference: the teacher asks students for hypotheses *before* they read each part of the text, inviting them to use their own experience and clues in the text to predict successive events. The emphasis on prediction in a DRTA raises the level of thinking about the text and engages students in critical evaluation of their hypotheses in light of the available evidence. The DRTA was introduced decades ago as the basic methodology of a published instructional program for students. For early discussions of the strategy as well as recent commentaries and applications, see the following selected readings: Stauffer, Burrows, and Horn (1960); Stauffer (1975); Nessel (1987); Davidson and Wilkerson (1988); Lenski, Wham, and Johns (1999); National Institute of Child Health and Human Development (2000); Taylor, Pressley, and Pearson (2002); and Dougherty-Stahl (2004).

Instructional Benefits of This Strategy

- activates prior knowledge
- arouses curiosity, increasing motivation to read
- leads students to have specific purposes for reading
- sharpens critical thinking and debating skills
- promotes active involvement in reading
- deepens and enhances comprehension of the material

Step by Step (Narrative Text)

To be successful with DRTAs, students need experience using clues to form hypotheses about upcoming events. They also should be able to debate different perspectives by listening to and responding directly to one another. When they are comfortable with these skills, here are the steps in conducting a DRTA with narrative text.

1. To prepare for the lesson, review the story and select three or four stopping points that will afford good opportunities for speculation about upcoming events. An effective stopping point is usually a critical juncture in the story when something important is about to happen.

2. At the start of the lesson, present the title and perhaps the first few sentences of the story and ask students what they think is going to happen next and why they think so. Elicit a few ideas and reasons, accepting each with a neutral comment such as "That's an interesting idea" or "Yes, that could happen."

3. Tell students they will be reading a little more of the story and stopping to make further predictions about what they think will happen next. Tell them they can't know for sure, because they have not read the whole story, but that they should be able to generate a few ideas based on what they know so far. Tell them where to stop, and have them mark the stopping point if you wish. Then have them continue reading.

4. At the first stopping point, guide the discussion with these questions:
   • What do you think will happen next?

   Accept all predictions with neutral responses. Not all students need give a prediction, but try to get several ideas so that students will realize that they are supposed to be engaged in divergent thinking.

   • Why do you think so?

   Have students explain why they think their ideas are plausible and cite as evidence what they have read in the story, their own firsthand experience, or what they have read elsewhere or seen on television. The discussion of reasons is as important to the development of critical thinking skills as is the generation of predictions.

   • Do you all agree? Why? Why not?

   This question encourages students to refine their thinking, evaluate their own and others' ideas, and decide if they will keep their original ideas or change their minds. Have students listen to each other and address each other directly as they debate their ideas. This aspect of the discussion, too, strengthens critical thinking skills.

5. After a few minutes of discussion, tell students it's time to read to get more information. Tell them the next stopping point and have them continue reading.

6. Ask students if they have found information relating to any of their predictions and have them discuss the information and read aloud from the text to support their assertions. Then repeat step 4.

7. Continue with the cycle of predict, read, discuss, predict, read, discuss until the group has finished the story. For long stories or novels, the DRTA may be extended over several lessons.

8. You may want to use one or more of the following questions in conducting a discussion at the end of the story:

    What was the most important part of the story to you? Why?

    Which character did you like the most? Why?

    Would you have acted differently than the characters did? How?

    What was the most surprising moment in the story to you? Why?

    What do you think would have happened if the story continued? Why?

Step by Step (Expository Text)

When students are comfortable with speculating and debating their ideas, here are the steps in conducting a DRTA with an expository text.

1. To prepare for the lesson, review the text and generate three or four questions that will afford good opportunities for speculation about the information contained in the text. For example, if the text is about daily life in ancient Egypt and has information about the sport the people most enjoyed, the pets they kept, and where they went for care when ill, questions might be:

    What do you think was the national sport in ancient Egypt?

    What animals do you think the ancient Egyptians kept as pets?

    Where do you think ancient Egyptians went when they became ill?

    The questions do not need to cover all the material in the text but should reflect some of the information that you consider important for students to remember or information that is especially interesting. The purpose of the prereading discussion is to stimulate curiosity and give students several specific purposes for reading.

2. At the start of the lesson, tell students the topic and pose the questions, one at a time. Tell them you don't expect them to know the answers but that you are interested in what they think. Encourage them to generate different responses and to debate their ideas. When students respond, use questions like these to probe their thinking:

   Why do you think so?

   How do you know that? (How reliable a source is that?)

   Do you all agree?

   Is there anything you might not have thought of?

   How sure are you of your hypotheses?

3. When students' curiosity has been piqued by the discussion, distribute the text and invite them to find information relevant to the questions and any other interesting information relating to the topic.

4. When students finish reading, facilitate a discussion about what they know now. Ask them to support their assertions by referring to the information in the text.

5. To bring closure to the lesson, use questions like these to help students summarize and reflect on the information they have acquired:

   What have we learned?

   How might we organize or picture this information to remember it?

   What was the most interesting piece of information you found?

   To what else does this information relate?

   What questions do you still have? What else would you like to know?

Additional Suggestions

- Students who are not familiar with prediction-oriented reading may express dissatisfaction when asked to speculate and may try to read ahead to get the answers quickly. At first, you may need to stress that it's important for them to learn to form and defend hypotheses, listen critically to others' ideas, cite evidence from texts, and develop the other high-level thinking skills that are an integral part of the strategy. With experience, most students come to enjoy the challenge and fun of the DRTA.

- For DRTAs with narrative texts, vary the number and kind of stopping points. For some stories, have students make their first predictions on the basis of the title alone or the title and an introductory illustration. For other stories, have them read the first page or two before generating predictions. Occasionally, have them read everything but the last page before they predict. Use the turning points in the story to decide where and how often to stop for predictions.

- For DRTAs with narrative texts, vary the way you present the text to students. Read the first part to them and stop for predictions (DLTA); then have them read the next part on their own. Or have them read and predict their way through most of the story, then read the last part aloud to them. Or have them read the first part as homework and bring in written predictions as preparation for the class discussion.

- For DRTAs with expository texts, pose questions that are answered in different parts of the text so that students will not find all the information they're looking for on the first page.

- For DRTAs with expository texts, divide long selections, such as chapters of a textbook, into parts and pose a few questions before students read each part.

- For students who are reluctant readers of expository texts you may wish not to mention at the outset that a reading assignment is forthcoming. Just engage them casually in discussing the questions so that they focus on the topic and not on the expectation that they will be reading to get information. The discussion is likely to arouse their curiosity enough that they will want to find the information and will approach the reading in a positive frame of mind.

  For example, one middle-school science teacher introduced a unit on thunderstorms on a day when the area was experiencing a violent thunderstorm. She had students discuss these questions one at a time, first in groups, then as a whole class:

  > What do you think causes the kind of thunder we've had today?

  > We saw some lightning earlier. Do you think a thunderstorm is always accompanied by lightning?

Do you think thunderstorms occur in all parts of the world?

Is it possible to have rain without having a thunderstorm?

Where do you think is the best place to be in a thunderstorm?

After a lively discussion, students then read information from several texts to learn more and discussed the questions again, using what they learned.

This approach is also suitable for primary-grade students who are about to listen to the teacher read an informational text. Discussing a few questions beforehand orients young children's attention to the topic, arouses their curiosity, and gives them specific purposes for listening. For example, a first-grade teacher was going to read students an informational picture book about firefighters. Knowing the students would see and hear the relevant information in the book, he had the class respond to these questions:

How many of you have seen firefighters racing through the streets, blowing their loud horns on the way to a fire? Let's talk about firefighters!

How do you think firefighters find out where there's a fire?

How long do you think it takes the firefighters to get in the truck and get moving once they get the alarm?

What do you think is some of the equipment a fire truck has?

What do you think is the most dangerous part of a firefighter's job?

As the teacher read the text aloud, he stopped periodically to have students respond to the information that was relevant to the questions to make sure that students now had the correct information.

7

Facts and Inferences

Overview and Background

Facts and Inferences helps students learn to distinguish between explicitly stated information and information that can be inferred from available evidence. The strategy involves them in generating a wide variety of inferences. With practice, they internalize a process of active, thoughtful reading that is beneficial when they read on their own. The strategy can be used at any grade level with a wide variety of materials, including narrative and expository texts, illustrations, charts, graphs, and videos.

Long before children attend school, they gain experience making inferences based on observations of their surroundings. For instance, they learn to infer other people's feelings from their facial expressions, and they learn to infer what adults are talking about by using clues from the conversation. Although all students have the capacity to apply this basic cognitive process to academic material, they may not do so readily. For any given listening or reading occasion, they may not understand the significance of the available evidence, may not have enough experience to bring to the situation, or may not realize that inferential thinking is expected of them.

Generations of researchers and teachers have recognized the importance of inferential thinking and have devised effective ways of giving students practice in "putting two and two together" to make an inference. Much classroom work on inferences, however, is limited to asking questions that call for specific inferences to be made. Facts and Inferences was devised by one of the authors to encourage students to infer without waiting to be prompted to make specific inferences. Although the strategy has been presented in handout form at numerous workshops presented by the authors, this is the first time it has been formally published. For further information about inferential thinking as a basic cognitive process and as a component of effective classroom instruction, see the following selected readings: Bruner (1973), Bransford (1979), Marzano and colleagues (1992), Keene and Zimmerman (1997), and Beers (2002).

Instructional Benefits of This Strategy

- develops the habit of inferential thinking
- refines and extends comprehension
- develops flexibility in thinking
- encourages students to learn from each other by listening to each other's responses
- encourages students to evaluate the plausibility of their responses, thereby increasing one aspect of their critical thinking abilities

---

Step by Step

To encourage students to generate and evaluate many ideas, organize them into groups of three or four and have them discuss their ideas within groups before sharing their best thinking with the whole class.

1. Choose or write a few simple sentences such as these, from which the explicitly stated information can be used to make one or more inferences:

   The sky darkened as gray clouds gathered overhead, and a strong wind began to blow. The people on the street opened their umbrellas.

2. Using the sentences, explain to students the difference between explicit and implicit information. Then model the

process of making an inference by saying something like this while highlighting the relevant words in the sentences:

> We know from the words that the sky is getting dark, gray clouds are forming, and the wind is blowing. We also know that people have opened their umbrellas. That's all explicit information: the information is stated directly. We can combine this explicit information with our own firsthand experience and infer that it has started to rain. The words don't say that it started to rain, but the evidence suggests that it has started to rain. That it has started to rain is implied; we infer this by connecting the available evidence with what we already know.

Put the examples on the board in a chart that looks like this:

Facts (Explicit Information)	Inferences (Implicit or Implied Information)
dark sky, gray clouds, wind blowing, umbrellas	It started raining.

Provide other such examples, with other simple texts, modeling how to identify explicitly stated information, combine it with experience, and generate an inference. Include these examples in the Facts and Inferences chart so that students become familiar with this way of displaying the information.

3. Choose or compose a longer text to work with, either one that students will read for themselves or one that you will read to them. Most students are at first better able to make inferences about characters and events than they are about factual information, so a narrative text that's unfamiliar to students is an effective choice at the start. Here is an example:

> Many years ago Conrad and Emily Hoffman lived on a dairy farm near a lake in the state of Iowa. They had chores on the farm just like all the other members of the Hoffman family. During some months of the year, they also attended a one-room school about two miles from their farm.
>
> Miss Johnson, the teacher, had been at the school for more than 30 years. She had taught Conrad's and Emily's mother and father and many of the other farmers in the area.

Everyone in the community liked Miss Johnson. The families often invited her to come to their homes for supper, and the mothers often sent their children to school with baskets of food for Miss Johnson from their own gardens.

4. Organize students into small groups, distribute copies of the text, and give each group a large piece of chart paper on which to create a Facts and Inferences chart for recording their ideas. Ask them to read the text, chart explicit information, and generate inferences that seem reasonable. Have groups post their charts in the room and take turns explaining their thinking. Here is a portion of a chart that might be generated from the passage about Conrad and Emily Hoffman:

Facts (Explicit Information)	Inferences (Implicit or Implied Information)
Conrad and Emily Hoffman lived with their family.	Conrad and Emily were siblings.
The Hoffmans had a dairy farm.	The Hoffman family had cows.
The Hoffmans did chores.	Conrad and Emily did farm chores. They may have milked cows, fed chickens, helped gather and prepare food, and so on.
Conrad and Emily went to school.	Conrad and Emily were not yet adults at this point in the story.
The school was two miles from the Hoffman home. The Hoffmans lived on a farm.	Conrad and Emily walked to school, or Conrad and Emily rode horses to school. (That the Hoffmans had horses is another inference.)
The school had one room.	Students of different ages attended the school. The school was small. There was only one class. The class was small.
Miss Johnson taught at the school for 30 years.	Miss Johnson was at least close to 50 years old at this point in the story.
Everyone liked Miss Johnson. Mothers sent food to Miss Johnson.	Mothers liked Miss Johnson. The families had more food than they needed for themselves. Miss Johnson was poor.

Acknowledge all inferences, including those that are debatable as well as those on which everyone agrees because they seem so credible. For example, highly credible inferences about the Hoffmans are that Conrad and Emily were brother and sister and that the Hoffman family had cows. A less credible inference is that Miss Johnson was poor. This can be logically inferred from knowing that the families provided Miss Johnson with meals and food baskets. However, it seems just as likely that the families treated Miss Johnson this way simply because they liked her, information that is also explicitly stated in the passage. Acknowledge and accept all these inferences so as to stimulate more inferential thinking. With practice, the quality as well as the quantity of students' inferences will improve.

5. When students are comfortable generating inferences in this way, increase the challenge by inviting them to rank their inferences according to how credible they are, discussing their reasons first in small groups and then as a whole class. This part of the process invites students to evaluate their ideas critically in light of the strength of the evidence in the text. No inferences need be discarded; the point is simply to recognize that the evidence supports some inferences more than others. For example, the evidence indicates only that Conrad and Emily share the last name of Hoffman and that they are among the members of the Hoffman family, so it could be inferred that they are cousins or are related to one another in some other way. However, it's more likely that they are brother and sister, given that in most stories featuring a boy and girl with the same last name, the children are siblings.

Additional Suggestions

- When students have had a number of experiences with narrative text, have them try to generate facts and inferences from expository text, such as science or social studies materials. For most students, this will be a more challenging task because they won't have extensive enough backgrounds of experience to make a large number of inferences. However, the exercise in thinking can be productive and interesting. For example, one group of students read an informational account about beavers that said the dam-building creatures gnaw at trees with their front teeth, and the students inferred that beavers must have extremely strong front teeth. Generating even a few such inferences when reading informational material encourages students to apply their inferential thinking skills to content-area material as well as to narrative literature.

- Use a photograph or an illustration as the text. Invite students to construct a Facts and Inferences chart based on what they see explicitly in the picture and what they can infer from what they see. Photographs of people in various situations, street scenes, and other interesting subjects encourage the same kind of inferential thinking in a different and, for some students, even more interesting context.

- When students are learning to interpret bar graphs in mathematics classes, they can use Facts and Inferences to organize the information shown in the bar graph and the inferences that they draw from the information. Here is an example of a simple graph created by elementary-school students to represent the results of a survey they took of students' preferences for main courses in the cafeteria.

Precentages of Students Who Prefer Different Cafeteria Foods

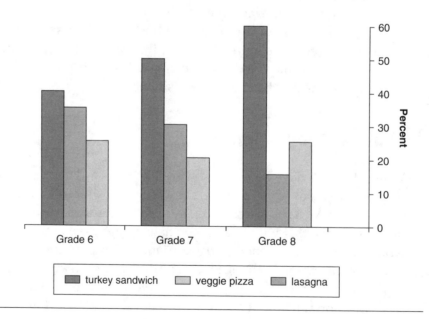

Here is the first part of the Facts and Inferences chart the students generated as they used the data to make inferences about food preferences at the school:

Facts (Explicit Information)	Inferences (Implicit or Implied Information)
40% of the 6th graders, 50% of the 7th graders, and 60% of the 8th graders liked the turkey sandwich.	The older the students get, the more they like the cafeteria's turkey sandwich.
35% of the 6th graders, 30% of the 7th graders, and 15% of the 8th graders liked the lasagna.	Cafeteria lasagna is less popular with the older students.

Just as some students may at first have difficulty putting two verbal statements together and making an inference that seems obvious to the teacher, they may also at first have difficulty putting different pieces of graphical information together to interpret meanings correctly. Children unfamiliar with bar graphs must learn how to put the information from the legend and the axes together with the information in the bars to draw correct conclusions. In the example, writing out the explicit information in the graph for the different grade levels and then putting the comparisons and trends in their own words helped students understand more clearly how to read and interpret data represented in a bar graph.

- Add a third column, labeled Opinions, to the Facts and Inferences chart. Using material that leads to the formation of opinions as well as the generation of inferences, encourage students to make distinctions among all three types of information. Here's an example of such an extension of the bar graph data:

Facts (Explicit Information)	Inferences (Implicit or Implied Information)	Opinions (What We Think)
40% of the 6th graders, 50% of the 7th graders, and 60% of the 8th graders liked the turkey sandwich.	The older the students get, the more they like the cafeteria's turkey sandwich.	The turkey sandwich is a lot better than the other two choices because they use really good bread.
35% of the 6th graders, 30% of the 7th graders, and 15% of the 8th graders liked the lasagna.	Cafeteria lasagna is less popular with the older students.	The lasagna isn't as good as it used to be at the school, and the portions are too small.

8

Frayer Model for Concept Development

Overview and Background

The Frayer Model for concept development helps students build a thorough understanding of a concept. The process involves contrasting examples of the concept with non-examples, determining essential and non-essential characteristics, and organizing the information into a chart (below). The accompanying discussion and debate stimulate high-level thinking, while the structuring of the ideas in writing aids comprehension and retention. Students respond best when they learn to use this strategy in conjunction with familiar concepts at a relatively low level of abstraction. At this level are such concepts as cat, house, or apple, examples of which are concrete and within the realm of the students' firsthand experience. After analyzing such concepts, students will be better able to move to higher levels of abstraction and analyze such complex concepts as lyrical poetry, immigration, Impressionism, mathematical equations, the life cycle, sportsmanship, or classical music.

Examples	Non-examples
What are some examples of _____? How may different examples can you think of?	What are some things that share some of the same characteristics as _____ and yet are not _____?

CONCEPT

Essential Characteristics	Non-essential Characteristics
What are the attributes or characteristics that every _____ must have?	What are some attributes or characteristics that some _____, but not all, may have?

Dorothy Frayer's work in cognitive psychology led her to develop this useful strategy for guiding students' concept learning. Her efforts are related to the earlier work of Jerome Bruner and others who saw concept attainment as a process of identifying the attributes or characteristics of the target concept, distinguishing examples that have similar attributes from those that don't, and defining the concept in terms of its essential attributes. Frayer's approach structures the collaborative inquiry and provides a model for students to use on their own. For early discussions of the strategy and the process of concept attainment along with recent commentaries and applications, see the following selected readings: Bruner, Goodnow, and Austin (1956); Frayer, Frederick, and Klausmeier (1969); Klausmeier, Ghatala, and Frayer (1974); and Buehl (2001).

Instructional Benefits of This Strategy

- develops, refines, and extends the understanding of a concept
- elicits and improves analytical thinking abilities
- develops skill in systematic organizing of information
- provides a visual tool that aids retention of information
- encourages collaborative pooling of knowledge to deepen understanding

Step by Step

The analysis of a simple concept at a low level of abstraction may be accomplished in one lesson, while the analysis of a complex concept at a higher level of abstraction may need to extend across several lessons. The suggested steps below can be modified to suit the ages and experience level of the students as well as the time available for the instruction.

1. Explain or remind students of the purpose of the strategy: to refine and deepen their understanding of a concept by engaging in a collaborative analysis of it.

2. Put the target concept in the middle of the chart. Give examples of what might be included in each category. Have students work both in small groups and as a whole class to think of examples and non-examples, essential characteristics and non-essential characteristics. They may discuss the four categories of information in any order and may add, delete, or revise information in any category at any time.

3. A discussion and the creation of the chart may be sufficient for some lessons. A more extensive activity may include having students write a definition using the information in the chart.

    Here is an example of a chart in progress, reflecting a discussion among students in a science class who are analyzing the concept *reptile:*

Examples	*Non-examples*
lizard	fish
snake	insect
iguana	chicken
frog	whale
gecko	
turtle	
REPTILE	
Essential Characteristics	*Non-essential Characteristics*
is cold-blooded	has multicolored skin
lays eggs	has fangs
has scales or plates on outside	lives in or near water
has a backbone	
has lungs	

Here is another example of a work in progress, reflecting a discussion among students in a mathematics class who are analyzing the concept *equation:*

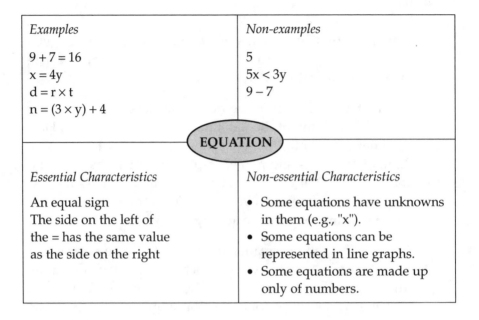

Examples	*Non-examples*
$9 + 7 = 16$ $x = 4y$ $d = r \times t$ $n = (3 \times y) + 4$	5 $5x < 3y$ $9 - 7$
Essential Characteristics An equal sign The side on the left of the = has the same value as the side on the right	*Non-essential Characteristics* • Some equations have unknowns in them (e.g., "x"). • Some equations can be represented in line graphs. • Some equations are made up only of numbers.

EQUATION

Additional Suggestions

- In the primary grades, have students use cut-out illustrations or their own drawings to represent examples and non-examples of the concept. For example, if the concept is *insect,* students can cut out or draw pictures of ants, beetles, ladybugs, and other insects for the EXAMPLES section of the chart. Pictures of lizards, birds, and other living things can be pasted in the NON-EXAMPLES section. At these grade levels, rather than asking students to identify "essential and non-essential characteristics" formally, they can be asked simply to talk about what all insects have in common (three pairs of legs, no backbone, etc.) and what only some insects have (spots, different colors, different habitats). These ideas can be included in the chart or not, as seems appropriate. For some groups, completing only the EXAMPLES and NON-EXAMPLES sections of the chart may be enough.

- When students in the secondary grades are familiar with the strategy, organize the class into Concept Groups and assign each group a different concept within a family of concepts. Have each group analyze its assigned concept, construct a Frayer Model chart to reflect their thinking, and share their work with the whole class. Keep the concept charts on display throughout the course of a unit so that the students can add to and revise the information as they learn more.

Here are a few examples of concept families in various content areas that would lend themselves to a Concept Group activity:

Science Concept Families	*Mathematics Concept Families*

Life Forms:
    mammal
    reptile
    insect
 	
Geographical Features:
    lake
    river
    estuary
    ocean
	Displays of Numerical Information:
	    area graph
	    line graph
	    bar graph
	    pie chart
	    table
	
	Measures of Central Tendency:
	    mean
	    median
	    mode

Language Arts Concept Families	*Social Studies Concept Families*

Types of Literature:
    poem
    short story
    novel
 	
Parts of Speech:
    noun
    verb
    adjective
    adverb
	Forms of Government:
	    federal republic
	    absolute monarchy
	    constitutional monarchy
	    totalitarian regime
	
	Wars:
	    American War for Independence
	    World War I
	    World War II
	    Vietnam War

- A variation on the Frayer Model involves leaving the concept area of the chart blank and having students figure out what the concept is from the information in the chart. This use of the chart gives students practice in inductive thinking while also developing their knowledge of the target concepts. When they are familiar with this activity, they can create their own "mystery concept" charts for one another. Here's an example:

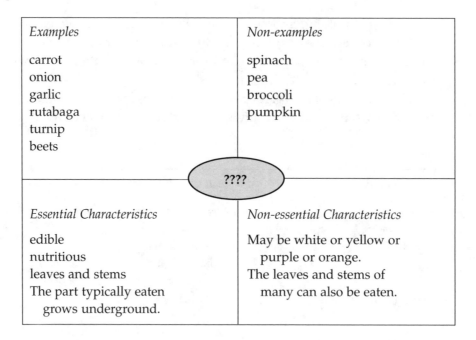

Examples	Non-examples
carrot onion garlic rutabaga turnip beets	spinach pea broccoli pumpkin
Essential Characteristics	*Non-essential Characteristics*

edible
nutritious
leaves and stems
The part typically eaten
  grows underground.
	May be white or yellow or
	  purple or orange.
	The leaves and stems of
	  many can also be eaten.

Answer: root vegetables

9

Freewriting

Overview and Background

Freewriting is a strategy that involves writing steadily without stopping and without worrying about mechanics for a predetermined period of time, usually somewhere between 2 and 10 minutes. Freewriting helps students collect their thoughts, explore associations with and reactions to a topic, formulate ideas, and improve their writing fluency. It can be used as a prewriting activity or as a way to determine how much a student knows about a given topic. Freewriting can be used in learning logs and journals or as way to generate ideas and thoughts that do not have to be shared. Freewriting may be focused or unfocused. If focused, the topic is determined before the writing begins; if unfocused, each student may choose a topic.

The concept of writing without stopping and without worrying about grammar, usage, or mechanics was advocated by Fader and Shaevitz (1966) and was named Freewriting by Elbow (1973). They stressed the value of this approach in helping writers develop fluency, confidence, and the sense that words are plentiful. By producing more, without worrying about style or conventions, writers are more likely to discover what they have to say and to later be better able to revise, edit, discard words, and sharpen the expression of their ideas. For many years, teachers have used Freewriting to help students understand how many practiced writers go about their craft. For early discussions of the strategy as well as recent commentaries and applications, see the following additional readings: Elbow (1981); Paznik-Bondarin and Baxter (1987); Decker-Collins (1990); Belanoff, Elbow, and Fontaine (1991); and Bomer (1995).

Instructional Benefits of This Strategy

- increases students' writing fluency
- helps students get started on a writing assignment
- generates ideas for writing
- provides an opportunity to formulate ideas
- builds confidence in writing
- accesses prior knowledge
- helps students review what they have learned
- promotes ease with editing

Step by Step

Explain the purpose of Freewriting to your students, telling them your goals for introducing it as a strategy. Model the process by doing a freewriting on the board while they watch. Make sure each student has paper or a journal in which to do his or her freewriting. Here are suggested guidelines for students for Unfocused Freewriting:

Student Guidelines for Unfocused Freewriting

1. Write for 3 to 5 minutes (or longer if you wish). Write whatever is on your mind.

2. Don't stop writing for any reason. Go steadily without rushing. If you can't think of something to write, write "Thinking" or another word until the ideas start to flow again.

3. Don't stop to look back, to cross something out, or to wonder how to spell any words.

4. If you can't think of a word or a spelling, just use a line or write, "I can't think of it."

5. Don't worry about how your writing sounds or looks, just keep on writing until the time is up.

For Focused Freewriting, use guidelines 2–5 above, but give students a topic and explain that they must stay with the topic for the time you allot them. Here are some examples of prompts that might be used in different curriculum areas. The key is to allow students some choice and to give them a prompt that's broad enough so that everyone can sustain writing about it for the expected amount of time.

Subject Area	Freewriting Topic Examples
Language Arts	Freewrite about a character in the story (novel) we're reading whom you would like to have as a friend.
Social Studies	Imagine that you were alive during the period of history we're studying. Freewrite about what your life would be like.
Science	Freewrite about one of the animals (concepts, systems) we've been studying.
Mathematics	Freewrite about a mathematical concept or type of problem we've been studying. (Examples might be multiplication, geometric shapes, time and distance problems, and ratio problems.)

Because the value of Freewriting lies in the process, not the result, teachers ordinarily do not collect or grade freewriting products, although they may give credit to the students for engaging in the activity for the expected period of time or for producing a certain amount of writing. Students may be encouraged to keep their freewritings, however, and use them for later reflection or glean from them ideas for the more formal writing that they do for specific audiences and other purposes.

Additional Suggestions

- Use Focused Freewriting in a content area as a means of evaluating students' prior knowledge of a specific topic. Collect their freewritings and read them to get an idea of the students' background with what you are about to teach.

- Introduce Freewriting as a method to think through the solving of math problems. Model the process for the class, then present a problem and have students freewrite in response, thinking aloud on paper as they figure out the solution. Have students share their freewritings by reading them aloud to partners or in small groups and discussing the strategies they used in solving the problem.

- Before a class discussion, allow students time to freewrite on the topic. The activity will help them orient their thinking and generate ideas. Then proceed with the discussion. Allow a few minutes at the end of the discussion for students to reflect on how Freewriting helped them prepare for participating in the discussion.

- Use a freewriting protocol to measure growth in fluency from one occasion to another. For example, give students a prompt to which everyone can easily respond, such as "Write as much as you can remember about being in ___ grade." Have them write for a specific amount of time. Have students count the number of words they wrote and enter the number at the top of their papers. Keep the papers. A month or two later, after regular practice with Freewriting, give them the same prompt, have them write for the same period of time, and again count the number of words they produced. Have students compare the prepractice and postpractice numbers, reflecting on any differences they notice.

10

Games for Thinking

Overview and Background

Having students systematically analyze a familiar game to understand its underlying principles is an excellent way to engage their thinking. A deeper understanding of a game also contributes to their sense of mastery of the game, which can, in turn, lead to greater satisfaction as a learner. Certain paper-and-pencil games can be used to sharpen students' observation and analysis skills when they study the game to discern underlying patterns and relationships.

A number of educators and educational researchers have advocated the use of various games and puzzles to develop problem-solving skills and critical thinking abilities. In this tradition are such simple games as Tic-Tac-Toe or Nim that are easy to learn and fun to play and that also afford students the opportunity to analyze patterns and strategies systematically by studying the game from new perspectives once the rules of play are familiar. For detailed examples and discussions of games that can be studied in this way, see Cornelius and Parr (1991). Useful sources for games are Solomon (1993) and Angiolino (1995). For an early discussion of the value of a variety of classroom games for enhancing thinking abilities and making learning more meaningful and enjoyable, see Abt (1970).

Instructional Benefits of This Strategy

- encourages inferential and analytical thinking
- refines observational skills
- develops skill in systematic observation and record keeping
- stimulates interest in logical thinking and problem solving

Step by Step

Before being successful with the analysis of a game, students need to understand the game thoroughly from the perspective of an ordinary player. It will also be helpful if they have had at least some experience carrying out systematic observations and organizing observed information clearly in charts so as to keep track of it.

1. Teach students the game and encourage them to play it with different partners until they become fully familiar with the rules and have had fun competing against each other.

2. Pose questions about the game that invite students to play cooperatively and analyze the moves in order to develop a deeper understanding of the game.

3. Have students write their observations as a collaborative summary of the analyses they completed.

The game "Sprouts," described by Cornelius and Parr (1991, pp. 44–46), will serve to illustrate. Two people or two teams play opposite each other. First, they set up the playing field by placing three small circles on the paper in any position. Side 1 draws a line to connect two of the circles and draws a new circle anywhere on the line. Side 2 responds by drawing a second line to connect two of the circles and placing a new circle anywhere on that second line. Play continues, in turn, until no additional moves can be made. The winner is the last one to make a legal move. Two constraints limit the moves. First, in drawing a line to connect two circles, a player may not cross an existing line. Second, when a circle has three lines emanating from it, that circle is out of play: no further lines can be drawn to or from it. In the game under way in the illustration, Player 1 connected circles A and B with a line and added circle D. Player 2 connected circle D to circle C and added circle E. As a result of that move, circle D is now out of play. The players shade it in to remind them of that.

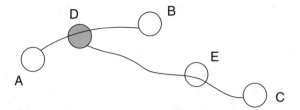

Questions that invite analysis of the game include these:

- Can the game continue on and on, or is there a finite number of moves that can be made?
- Is there a clear strategy for winning if you make the first move? The second move?
- What happens if the players start with 2 circles? 4 circles? 5 circles? Other numbers of circles?
- Do you see any pattern in the outcomes of the games as the number of circles increases?

NOTE: The game does have a finite number of moves. When n equals the number of circles at the start, the number of moves possible in a game will fall between $2n$ and $(3n-1)$. The actual number of moves and the outcome depend on the specific moves that are made and where the lines are drawn.

Additional Suggestions

- For both competitive and cooperative play, have students play as individuals first, then as pairs or teams of three playing opposite other pairs or teams. Encourage students to observe and comment on the change in the dynamics when they play cooperatively instead of competitively.

- As students study the game and write up their observations, have pairs or groups share their findings with one another, either by posting their work or by sharing their discoveries orally.

- Played cooperatively, "Sprouts" and other games can be used to provide practice in using the scientific method. Students observe the play itself and track the moves systematically from one game to the next, noticing what happens. They then form hypotheses about how they might change the moves they make to keep the game going longer or find a winning strategy. Then they test their hypotheses by playing the game again. Their game notes are comparable to science lab notes; their conclusions stem from the sequence of careful observations they make as they test their various hypotheses.

- Use several games that lend themselves to the same kind of critical analysis. Introduce a new game every few weeks to keep interest high. With practice, students will improve their analytical skills and their ability to organize and write an analysis of a game that includes discernment of essential patterns and an under-standing of the underlying principles of the game. The sources cited above include many such games that are suitable for play at different grade levels.

11

Graphic Organizers

Overview and Background

A graphic organizer is used to arrange information on a page so that the relationships among the concepts are made clear visually. For instance, a causal relationship might be shown with arrows pointing from causes to effects, or subordinate details might be shown radiating from a main idea like spokes from the center of a wheel. For some learners, information is easier to process if the ideas are arranged graphically instead of in a linear fashion, as is the case with traditional outlines, lists, or pages of notes. For most learners, such visual displays can be aids to comprehension and retention of information.

There are many different types of graphic organizers. The one to choose depends on the relationships that are inherent in the material or the relationship on which students are asked to focus. For example, the Venn diagram, developed by John Venn in the 1880s, was first used in mathematics to show the relationship between elements in a set. Venn diagrams are now used in every area of the curriculum to illustrate similarities and differences between two or more people, ideas, or items. A T-chart is used to organize information about two topics or main ideas. A flowchart with boxes and arrows, commonly seen in the business world to lay out a plan of action, can be used in the classroom to organize information into chronological order, either from left to right or from top to bottom, while boxes and arrows can also be used to show specific cause-effect relationships.

Research shows that when students use graphic organizers their comprehension and learning increase. Dunston (1992) found that students who constructed graphic organizers after reading had increased achievement scores and improved recall. Hyerle (1996, 2000) provides many examples of effective uses of such learning aids and argues persuasively for the use of visual tools that are linked to specific thinking processes. Marzano, Pickering, and Pollock (2001) present the demonstrated value of having students make nonlinguistic representations of what they have learned so as to deepen their understanding. Experienced teachers use graphic aids with students at all grade levels to facilitate learning across all content areas. For early discussions of the strategy as well as recent commentaries and applications, see the following selected readings: Baird and White (1984); Moore and Readance (1984); Dunston (1992); Bromley, Modlo, and Irwin-De Vitis (1995); Hyerle (1996, 2000); and Marzano and colleagues (2001).

Instructional Benefits of This Strategy

- helps students understand relationships among ideas
- refines and extends comprehension of information
- helps students see learned information from a new perspective
- provides students with an independent study strategy
- refines and extends the kind of thinking required to construct the organizer

Step by Step

1. Show students how to organize ideas in a graphic organizer so that they understand how to proceed. Use material from a recent lesson so that students are familiar with the vocabulary and concepts and can concentrate on seeing the relationships and understanding how to display them graphically. Here are some examples:

    Example 1: Comparing and Contrasting Fictional Characters A and B With a Venn Diagram

The teacher drew the Venn diagram on the board, explained to students where the categories of information would go, and first had students meet in small groups to discuss aspects of two characters from a novel they were reading. Next, groups reported the results of their discussions, and as they mentioned character traits, the teacher put the information in the appropriate places in the diagram, as shown here.

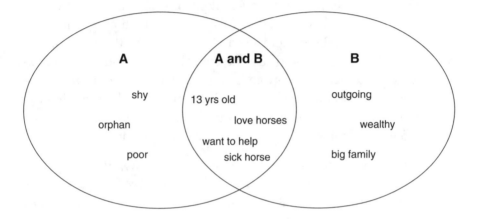

Example 2: Organizing Main Ideas and Details Into a T-Chart

The teacher drew a T-chart on the board and wrote in two main ideas about a topic students had been discussing recently. Students met in small groups to generate details, and when they reported their ideas, the teacher wrote them on the T-chart in the appropriate places.

Main Idea 1 : Doubles tennis is fun.	*Main Idea 2:* Doubles tennis teaches cooperation.
Detail 1: more people playing	Detail 1: take turns at net and in back court
Detail 2: usually faster	Detail 2: can set up shots for partner
Detail 3: better net shots	Detail 3: both players are responsible

2. Model for students how to use the information in the organizer for an appropriate learning purpose, such as a study aid or as a way of organizing a response to a test question. In Example 1, the teacher modeled for students how to design a computerized

presentation that compared and contrasted the two characters, using the information in the Venn diagram. In Example 2, the teacher modeled how to present each main idea as a topic sentence in a paragraph, using the details from the T-chart as support.

3. After constructing a few graphic organizers with students and showing them how to use the completed organizer for a specific purpose, put them in small groups, and give each group a blank organizer to go with a reading (listening, viewing) assignment. Have them work together to fit the information into the structure and use the completed organizer for a specific purpose, for example, as a study aid. Have groups share their work and discuss any differences in their completed organizers. Do this several times until students are comfortable using the organizing structures you provide.

4. Let students practice constructing their own graphic organizers in small groups to accomplish specific learning purposes. For example, the class that learned to use a Venn diagram as the basis for designing a computerized compare–contrast presentation was given several additional assignments to construct and use a Venn diagram to design similar presentations to compare and contrast characters from other works of literature they had studied as a class. The class that learned to use a T-chart to organize main ideas and details was given several additional assignments that involved constructing a T-chart and writing similarly structured paragraphs on other topics.

5. After providing students with information, such as a selection to read or a video, have students work in small groups to decide how they could organize the information graphically. Have groups share their organizers and discuss the kinds of thinking that went into their decisions. Do this several times with different texts to give students practice in deciding for themselves how to organize information graphically.

6. Give students opportunities to use graphic organizers in different content areas so that they have practice using these visual aids in various contexts. For example, here are other possible uses for Venn diagrams and T-charts:

Content Area	Suggested Use for Venn Diagram
Literature	Compare/contrast stories, characters, poems, literary techniques, or themes
Math	Compare/contrast numbers, geometric shapes, rules, or computational processes
History	Compare/contrast persons, events, forms of government, or eras
Science	Compare/contrast observable organisms or phenomena, competing theories, scientific laws, or famous scientists

Content Area	Suggested Use for T-Chart
Literature	Generate statements about characters in a literary work that are supported by details from the work
Math	Generate statements about geometric shapes (or other mathematical phenomena) that are supported by specific examples
History	Generate statements about persons, events, forms of government, or eras that are supported by specific examples
Science	Generate statements about observable organisms or phenomena, scientific laws, or branches of scientific inquiry that are supported by specific examples

Additional Suggestions

- At the end of a unit of study, have students work in small groups to summarize what they learned in a graphic organizer of their own choosing. Have groups share their work and the reasons they chose the specific graphic organizer.

- Have students use a T-chart to organize the advantages and disadvantages of a particular decision. The organized information can be used as the basis of a persuasive speech or essay or to prepare for a class debate.

- Have students explain how they solved a math problem by using a flowchart that details each step they took and the thinking they did at that point.

- Have students write a brief account comparing two topics, such as historical figures, kinds of plants and animals, or literary selections. Collect their papers and put them aside. Then, working with the whole class, use a Venn diagram to guide students in comparing and contrasting the same two topics. Return to students' accounts and have them revise using the ideas from the graphic organizer. Have students discuss the ways in which the graphic organizer helped them improve their thinking and writing.

- Instead of giving students an essay question on a test, ask them to show what they know by constructing an appropriate graphic organizer. This can be an effective alternate way to assess student's understanding of a concept or process and is especially effective for students who have difficulty expressing themselves in writing.

12

I-Search Reporting

Overview and Background

An I-Search report is an original piece of expository writing that's based on a question the writer poses and then answers by researching information. The research may include interviews and observations as well as the use of print and electronic sources. Such reports are ordinarily written in the first person and are usually conversational in tone and approach. This approach to reporting encourages students to write in their own words and present information from their own perspective rather than copy it from an encyclopedia or another source. The I-Search report also gives students excellent opportunities to develop critical thinking skills as they judge the validity and reliability of the sources they use and the relevance of the information they find to the question(s) they posed.

I-Search Reporting was designed by Ken Macrorie as an alternative to reports based on print-based sources of information. Several elements of the I-Search approach appeal to students: they choose their topic, they investigate answers to questions they pose themselves, they select and use a variety of sources of information, and they write in their own way to describe the search they undertook and convey what they learned about something of genuine interest to them. For early discussions of I-Search Reporting along with recent commentaries and applications, see the following selected readings:

Macrorie (1976, 1988), Shafer (1999), Wilson and Castner (1999), Bowen (2001), and Wachsberger (2005). For earlier perspectives on the value of student-centered inquiry, see Kelley (1947), Postman and Weingartner (1969), Moffett (1973), and Stauffer (1969, 1975).

Instructional Benefits of This Strategy

- allows report writing to grow from students' own interests and purposes
- develops research and reporting skills
- develops critical thinking skills related to evaluation of source material
- stimulates interesting, original expository writing
- prepares students for writing more formal research reports that are based on reading
- refines and extends general writing abilities

Step by Step

1. Have students identify an interest and formulate questions about it related to their concerns and pursuits. For instance, a student who has just obtained a new pet may want to learn about the animal and how to care for it. One who is designing a Web site may have some technical questions pertaining to desired effects or functions. Students of a specific ethnic background may have questions about the history and culture of their people. Here are some interests and questions to illustrate the kinds of response you might expect from students:

Interest	Questions
We're going to Yellowstone National Park this summer.	What things can I see and do there? What's the weather like? What do the park rangers do? How many geysers are there at Yellowstone?
I like hip-hop music.	What are the origins of the music? What are the major themes represented in the music?
I want to have a vegetable garden.	What do I need to know to be successful? What would be the best vegetables to plant? How many seed packets do I need?

I'm interested in designing computer games.	What is involved in designing a computer game? What do I need to do to get into that kind of work?
I just learned about magic squares in math class.	Did mathematical magic squares really come from Asia? What's their history?
I like soccer.	Who have been the best players through the years? Why were they considered the best?

As students identify interests and formulate questions, help them narrow queries that are very broad or add related questions that will enhance their learning. For instance, the question above about the best soccer players in the past is enhanced with the question relating to why they were considered the best, whereas the one about how to grow a vegetable garden is too broad. Better might be, What do I need to know to grow good tomatoes?

2. Have students work in pairs or groups to make lists of possible sources of information. Provide suggestions and help as needed, reminding them that the best sources include people who know about their topic, organizations that can be visited or reached by phone, television or radio programs and podcasts, as well as Web sites, magazines, newspapers, and books from the library. Encourage students to use nonprint sources as much as possible, even exclusively, so that they will learn that research involves more than looking things up in encyclopedias or on the Internet.

3. Allow time for students to gather information and take notes over the course of several days or longer. Have them keep their questions with them as they search. If they have more than one question, have them organize their notes by question.

4. When students are ready to write their drafts, have them write in the first person, as if they are simply talking to someone about what questions they had, whom they consulted, what they did to find the answers, and what they discovered. When students adopt such a conversational tone, they naturally write what they learned in their own words. This can help

them when they later report information they obtain from reading. Also, by asking students to include an account of the search itself in the report, they will be able to complete the assignment even if they did not find answers to their questions. Here are two examples of the beginnings of two first drafts of I-Search reports.

> I'm interested in having a vegetable garden, so I started by thinking about tomatoes. My mom told me that a lady on our block grows tomatoes every year, so I went to talk to her. She showed me all of her plants—all 25 of them! And she said she would be happy to give me some tips. "Tomatoes are not hard to grow," she said, "but you need to know a few things to get a good crop."
>
> She told me to start with little tomato plants because they are a lot easier than starting with seeds. . . .

> There's a lot more to being a computer game designer than I thought. I wanted to know what training I needed, so I talked to my neighbor, Collin Blake, who designs computer games. He said I needed to learn a lot about computer graphics and computer programming. He also showed me his favorite book of math and logic puzzles. "The kind of thinking you need to do puzzles like these is the kind of thinking I do a lot in my work: careful, step-by-step reasoning." . . .

5. Have students meet in small groups to help each other revise their drafts to improve clarity of expression, use of supporting details, word choice, and anything else that's important in terms of the goals for written expression you have for the class.

6. Have students publish their I-Search reports by posting them around the classroom, in the hallway, or on the school's or district's Web site. You may also want to have students present their findings orally. Keep copies of their reports to use as examples for the next time you use the strategy or to share with other classes.

Additional Suggestions

- Students in the primary grades can use a simplified version of the I-Search process. Individuals can each pose one question they would like to answer and can search for information at home, within their families, and in their neighborhoods. They can share their findings orally in class and, as a culminating activity, write or draw a simple summary of something they learned.

- Establish a Question Wall in your room where students can write interesting questions at any time. When it's time for an I-Search assignment, some students may want to mine the Question Wall for ideas.

- Maintain an ongoing list of your students' I-Search topics and questions for your own records and for reviewing with students periodically. Have students evaluate the questions they asked at different points in the year. Encourage them to comment on the questions and on the question-asking skills they are developing.

- When students are familiar with I-Search Reporting, challenge them to pose questions that they consider more difficult than usual but that are still grounded in their genuine interests. For example, the student who learned more about growing tomatoes may be interested in investigating varieties of heirloom tomatoes, and the student who learned about the geysers at Yellowstone National Park may be interested in learning about geysers elsewhere in the world or about the use of geothermal power.

13

Imitation Writing

Overview and Background

When students engage in Imitation Writing, they follow (or imitate) the structure or pattern of a model. The model can be a sentence, a paragraph, a poem, or some other piece of writing that's either selected from an existing work or composed by the teacher. The process involves four steps:

1. Read the model carefully.

2. Copy the model word for word.

3. Substitute synonyms for as many words as possible.

4. Write on a different topic using the same syntactical structure as the model.

The expectation that the imitation must closely follow the model leads to high-level thinking as well as creativity. In order to imitate closely, the writer must analyze the structure of the model, adhere to the constraints of the structure, evaluate his or her attempt to see if it follows the pattern correctly, and make appropriate revisions as needed.

Imitation Writing is based on a simple premise: Students can improve their writing by imitating writing produced by more practiced writers. The process of imitation has been used formally and informally in a variety of endeavors for many years. To refine their craft and hone their skills, novice painters, filmmakers, craftsmen, and others study and, at first, sometimes imitate the style of accomplished people in their respective fields. Similarly, students can improve their expressive skills by studying well-crafted sentences and paragraphs and using them as models for their own writing. The strategy of Imitation Writing has been in the repertoire of many experienced teachers for decades because of the opportunities it affords for high-level thinking as well as for refining writing skills. For early discussions of the strategy as well as recent commentaries and applications, see the following selected readings: Moffett (1973), Greene (1991), Butler (2002), and Hillebrand (2004).

Instructional Benefits of This Strategy

- improves writing versatility and expressiveness
- challenges creative thinking and writing within a fixed structure
- increases understanding of sentence and paragraph structure
- encourages analysis of language structures
- refines reading comprehension ability
- develops reading and writing vocabularies
- establishes a base for learning grammar concepts

Step by Step

1. Write the model or choose one from an existing source. The model should be challenging but not too difficult for the students. A short, simple sentence will be appropriate for primary-grade students or for students who haven't done this activity before. For example:

   The gray cat crept softly across the grass.

   Ricky ate his lunch and drank his milk.

   A sentence of greater syntactical complexity will be appropriate for older or more experienced writers. For example:

   Sonora, a dancer, is the pride of her family.

   The gulls on the wharf were loud, hungry, and aggressive.

   On the wall near the door hung a crayon drawing of a skunk and a raccoon.

2. Work with the model yourself first to see if you can generate several imitations. If you can compose several sentences in imitation of the model, then your students will probably be able to think of others. Some sentences or paragraphs are easier than others to imitate. If you can't easily imitate a sentence, your students probably won't be able to either.

3. Model the four steps in the process for the whole class, thinking aloud and composing while they watch. For example, put the sentence on the board and say:

   Look at this sentence as I read it to you.
   (Read aloud to class.)

   The gray kitten crept softly across the grass.

   Read it with me. (Have students read with you in unison.)

   Now watch how I copy the sentence. (Copy the sentence directly underneath the original and again read it aloud.)

   The gray kitten crept softly across the grass.
   The gray kitten crept softly across the grass.

   Now I'm going to substitute synonyms for the key words. (Write a substitution sentence.)

   The gray kitten crept softly across the grass.
   The gray kitten crept softly across the grass.
   The smoky cat moved quietly across the lawn.

   Now I'm going to write exactly the same kind of sentence, but I'm going to change the topic. (Write one or more imitation sentences.)

   The gray kitten crept softly across the grass.
   The gray kitten crept softly across the grass.
   The smoky cat moved quietly across the lawn.
   The spotted dog ran wildly down the street.
   A cheerful robin sang brightly in the tree.

4. Have students work in pairs or small groups to compose more sentences in imitation of the model and then share their sentences with the whole class by writing them on the board or on overhead transparencies so that everyone can see the sentences as well as hear them. Here are some student imitations of the

pattern shown in the example. They were collected in class-rooms from primary grades through high school:

The angry lion roared loudly in the jungle.

The coral snake moved silently through the leaves.

The sleeping dog snored softly by the fire.

A wild parrot flew quickly above the treetops.

A beautiful peacock strutted proudly across the lawn.

An expert skater sped rapidly across the ice.

The industrious student read diligently into the night.

5. To challenge students to think more carefully about sentence structure, point out any deviations from the model they may have created, and guide them to revise in order to match the model. For example, consider this attempted imitation generated by a small group of first graders:

ORIGINAL: The gray kitten crept softly across the grass.

IMITATION: The excited dog ran around the house and barked.

The teacher guided them to see how to revise their sentence to follow the structure of the original:

REVISED: The barking dog ran excitedly around the house.

6. The model and the sentences the students create can also be used to develop grammar concepts. For instance, the example sentence can be used to teach prepositional phrases or the concept of an adverb as a modifier of a verb.

Additional Suggestions

- In the primary grades, books with simple, predictable text are excellent models for Imitation Writing. Students can create their own books that follow the same syntactic and rhyming patterns. The book *Brown Bear, Brown Bear, What Do You See?* (1967) by Bill Martin, Jr., is one example of such a book.

- In the primary grades, students can compose their imitations orally as you record their words on the board or chart paper. Put the model sentence on the board, read it aloud a few times, and have the students read it with you until they are familiar with the sentence. Then have them generate their own sentences orally. You may want to structure their composing to insure their success, building the sentence one part at a time. For example, here is the exchange between a teacher and some first-grade students who worked together to imitate the example sentence: The gray kitten crept softly across the grass.

Speaker	Dialogue	On the Board
Teacher	Let's write an imitation of the sentence. What animal should we write about?	
Students	A hamster!	
Teacher	All right.	hamster
Teacher	The cat was gray. What word can we use to describe the hamster?	
Students	Friendly.	
Teacher	That's a good descriptive word.	friendly hamster
Teacher	What word do we need in front of friendly hamster? Look at the model for a clue.	
Students	The!	
Teacher	Right.	The friendly hamster
Teacher	The kitten crept. What did the friendly hamster do?	
Students	It ran!	
Teacher	OK.	The friendly hamster ran
Teacher	The kitten crept across the grass. Where did the hamster run?	
Students	Around the cage.	
Teacher	That's a good idea!	The friendly hamster ran around the cage.

- In the upper grades, Imitation Writing can be applied in social studies units using sentences or passages from famous historical speeches, such as Abraham Lincoln's *Gettysburg Address* ("Fourscore and seven years ago . . ."), Franklin Roosevelt's first inaugural address ("The only thing we have to fear is fear itself"), or the "I Have a Dream" speech Martin Luther King, Jr. delivered in front of the Lincoln Memorial in 1963.

- To help students in mathematics become more aware of the structural patterns and conventions of wording within word problems, have them compose new word problems based on existing problems. For example:

ORIGINAL: Martin and James each had three quarters. In addition, Martin had two dimes, and James had four nickels. How much money did they have altogether?

IMITATION: Maria and Penny each had five dimes. In addition, Maria had three quarters, and Penny had two pennies. How much money did they have altogether?

- When focusing on grammar, use a sentence that illustrates a specific concept in grammar or a rule of punctuation. After students complete their imitations, identify the sentences that adhere to the pattern. Ask students to study these and state the concept or rule they imitated in their own words. For example, here are three examples that illustrate a rule of punctuation:

The team played in the rain, and the loyal spectators stayed.

The car raced around the track, and the excited fans cheered.

The band played into the night, and the enthusiastic guests danced.

Student-generated rule: When two sentences are connected by *and*, put a comma after the first sentence.

Such inductive reasoning to determine a rule can help students learn and remember the rule more effectively.

- Use unusual syntactical patterns to challenge students' thinking and writing skills. For example, this sentence is from the beginning of J.R.R. Tolkien's *The Hobbit* (1937):

ORIGINAL: In a hole in the ground there lived a hobbit.

COPY: In a hole in the ground there lived a hobbit.

SUBSTITUTION: In a hollow in the earth there resided a hobbit.

IMITATE: At the top of a mountain there perched an eagle.

                Under the eaves of a roof there nested a squirrel.

The sentence below was composed for an imitation writing lesson in a high school English class. The students, who were familiar with the strategy, focused on imitation and so did not write substitution sentences.

ORIGINAL: To sail through the bright blue water of the Aegean Sea is an exhilarating experience.

IMITATIONS: To lie on the creamy white sand of a Florida beach is an extraordinary pleasure.

                To climb up the rough rock face of a Yosemite cliff is a distinct challenge.

                To dance on the polished wood floor of a New York stage is a terrific thrill.

14

Jigsaw

Overview and Background

Jigsaw learning was developed by Elliott Aaronson and a group of graduate students in 1971. Each student is responsible for learning one aspect of a selected topic in depth and then teaching it to others. The development of this way of learning came out of the need to promote positive race relations in recently integrated classrooms in Austin, Texas. Jigsaw learning was used to bring about a climate of cooperation and to build interdependence. Use of the strategy developed a sense of teamwork in students while they acquired new knowledge or reviewed previous learning.

Studies showed that after using Jigsaw for only a short period of time students reported that they liked school more, expressed less prejudice toward others, and were more confident as learners. In addition, students were absent less often and showed greater academic growth than students not using Jigsaw (Aaronson, Blaney, Stephen, Sikes, & Snapp, 1978). Repeated use of the strategy since then has confirmed that it is also effective in helping students refine and extend their thinking about curriculum material because of the effort they put into figuring out how to teach the material to others.

Students start out in a "home" group and are then reassigned to an "expert" group, each member of the home group going to a different expert group. In their expert groups, students help each other master one segment of the assigned material and figure out together how to teach the material to their home groups. According to Robb (2003), the strategy works best with materials that involve learning new concepts and covering large amounts of unfamiliar ideas and vocabulary, as is often the case in science, social studies, or literature classes.

Instructional Benefits of This Strategy

- develops a sense of teamwork
- increases interaction
- builds individual accountability
- fosters cooperation
- fosters discussion
- builds negotiating and decision-making skills
- builds comprehension
- builds listening and speaking skills

Step by Step

1. Divide the reading material into segments, depending on the number of groups you want to organize in your class. For example, if you have 30 students, you might have six groups of five students each. Groups should be diverse in terms of achievement level, ethnicity, English-language skills, and gender.

2. Organize students into groups, explain the purpose of Jigsaw, and distribute the materials students will be reading. Have students number off within their groups. For example, in each group of five, the students will number off 1 through 5,

3. Have students move into expert groups. All the 1's will be in one group, all 2's in another group, and so on.

4. Allow students time to read the material at least twice before they begin their discussions with other expert-group members. The first reading could be a homework assignment, while the second reading could be done in class with the expectation that students will take notes as they reread.

5. Allow time for students to discuss the material and determine what and how they will present what they have learned to

their home groups. Students should rehearse their presentations and help each other until all are sure they can teach the material to their home groups.

6. Have students return to their home groups, where they will now take turns teaching what they learned in their expert groups. Move among the groups to observe and monitor the process.

7. When the teaching is complete, conduct a debriefing on the activity. How did it work? What did they learn about themselves? What did they learn about working in a group? How can they improve the next time they use Jigsaw?

8. Discuss the information with the class as a whole to check on their comprehension, discuss questions students might have, and clear up any misconceptions.

Additional Suggestions

- Use Jigsaw for exploring different points of view on controversial issues. Each expert group can focus on a different perspective in its reading and viewing. For example, in the westward movement in American history, the guiding question might be, Was the westward expansion of the 19th century a positive force on the growth and development of the United States of America? One expert group can focus on the pioneer farmers who sought land; another group can focus on the native peoples whose land was desired by the pioneer farmers; another group can focus on the United States government, which sought to develop policies advantageous to the growing country; another group can focus on the governments of Mexico and Canada, which had their own concerns about the United States' growth, and so on. When the members of the expert groups return to their home groups, the home groups can discuss the guiding question with greater appreciation for the complexity of the issues involved.

- Give expert groups different materials on which to base their learning. For example, in learning about the history of African American people in the United States, each expert group can study one or more different texts: a poem, a nonfiction book, a textbook chapter, part of a novel, a video, song lyrics, and recent magazine articles. When the home groups come together to discuss the topic, each member will have information from a different text to bring to the discussion.

- Assign each expert group a different section in the textbook chapter in order to review the class's work on that chapter. Robb (2003) specifically recommends this use of Jigsaw for reviewing math content.

- In any class, have each expert group prepare drawings and diagrams as presentation aids that group members will use for teaching in their respective home groups. For example, in a science lesson on different species, expert groups might prepare a presentation that includes detailed, labeled drawings of the different species.

- Use the Jigsaw strategy when having students explore a specific genre or author in a literature unit. For example, to engage an elementary-school class in a study of the author Patricia Polacco, assign each expert group a different book by this author, as shown here:

Expert Group 1	Expert Group 2	Expert Group 3	Expert Group 4	Expert Group 5
My Rotten Redheaded Older Brother	Thank You, Mr. Falker	Chicken Sunday	Rechenka's Eggs	Picnic at Mudsock Meadow

Have each expert group cooperatively collect the following information as they read the book and prepare to take it to their respective home groups:

Characters (Who are the people in the story?)

Setting (Where does the story take place?)

Problem (What is the main problem the characters face?)

Events (What happened as the characters tried to solve their problem?)

Solution (How did the problem get solved?)

Illustrations (How did the pictures help tell the story?)

When the home groups reconvene, each member will have information about a different book, and all five books will be represented in each home group, as shown here.

Home Group 1	Home Group 2	Home Group 3	Home Group 4	Home Group 5
My Rotten Redheaded Older Brother	My Rotten Redheaded Older Brother	My Rotten Redheaded Older Brother	My Rotten Redheaded Older Brother	My Rotten Redheaded Older Brother
Thank You, Mr. Falker	Thank You, Mr. Falker	Thank You, Mr. Falker	Thank You, Mr. Falker	Thank You, Mr. Falker
Chicken Sunday	Chicken Sunday	Chicken Sunday	Chicken Sunday	Chicken Sunday
Rechenka's Eggs	Rechenka's Eggs	Rechenka's Eggs	Rechenka's Eggs	Rechenka's Eggs
Picnic at Mudsock Meadow	Picnic at Mudsock Meadow	Picnic at Mudsock Meadow	Picnic at Mudsock Meadow	Picnic at Mudsock Meadow

Have students report the information they collected in their expert groups, and then have students identify and discuss common characteristics across all five books. Each home group can record their responses on a chart and share these with the whole class. Finally, engage the whole class in a discussion of the characteristics of Patricia Polacco's writing and illustrating style.

15

Journals and
Learning Logs

Overview and Background

A journal is an individual notebook in which a student writes freely. When the purpose is primarily to write about specific information that is being learned, the journal may be called a learning log.

Ordinarily, journals are used for private observations and reflections that even the teacher does not read. Students write about their daily lives, examining their relationships with others and the world, their reactions to important events, and their thoughts about any topic. In contrast, learning logs are used for class notes, reflections on learning, and other such purposes related to lessons. The writing is usually considered to be public. That is, students would expect to share what they write with the teacher or peers.

Journals and learning logs have been used for decades at all grade levels across the curriculum. They provide a place for students to summarize and reflect on ideas and an efficient way for students to organize and keep all of their notes for a specific content area in one place. They encourage students to sort out experiences, solve problems, and consider varying perspectives. As students progress through the school year, journals and learning logs serve as evidence of their academic and personal growth. For early discussions of the strategy as well as recent commentaries and applications, see the following selected readings: Britton, Burgess, Martin, McLeod, and Rosen (1975); Emig (1977); Geeslin (1977); Fulweiler (1980); Atwell (1989); Bomer (1995); Norwood and Carter (1996); Rester-Zodrow and Chancer (1997); Vacca and Vacca (2002); and Wolf (2004).

Instructional Benefits of This Strategy

- increases writing fluency and comfort with writing
- helps students think of themselves as writers
- reinforces and enhances learning
- enables students to examine and reflect on relationships with others
- encourages students to solve problems and summarize ideas, experiences, and opinions before and after instruction
- allows students to reflect on academic and personal growth by reading past entries

Step by Step

1. Decide on the type of journal or learning log you want your students to keep. Several common types are described below.

2. Provide each student with a journal. Journals can be as simple as several sheets of paper stapled together or can be sturdy booklets purchased from a store.

3. Establish a journal-writing routine and stick to it. Set aside a time of day for journal writing and establish a schedule: for example, every day, every other day, or once or twice a week. Post the schedule to remind yourself and students to do it.

4. Establish guidelines for using journals. For example:
   - Write every day.
   - Write for at least 15 minutes.
   - Write at least three sentences (or a page, or some other criterion).

5. If you have established the journal or learning log as a place for public writing, plan time to have students share their entries and discuss or respond to one another's ideas. If the journal is to be private, allow occasional time for students to reread earlier entries and reflect on them privately.

6. Keep a journal yourself and share its contents with your students. Writing in front of students provides an effective model for them and demonstrates that you value the activity.

   The type of journal or learning log you choose to use in your classroom will depend upon the type of material with which you are working. Character journals, double-entry journals, reader response journals, and learning logs each provide unique opportunities for active learning and are discussed in detail below.

Character Journal. A character journal is a written diary kept by a reader as he or she assumes the role of the main character of a book being read (Hancock, 1993). Students can also keep a character journal in a social studies, science, or math class as they learn about the lives of explorers, scientists, or mathematicians.

1. Model one or more character-journal entries for the entire class before asking students to keep their own. Use books that have strong main characters, preferably about the same age as your students. You may also have students select someone they are learning about in the content areas.

2. Read a chapter or two a day with or to your class. Then collaborate to write a journal entry in the character's "voice." Include a personal response (in a different color) after the character's entry.

3. After you and your class have kept a character journal together for a while, have individuals keep their own. Provide a range of book titles and let students choose their own book and character. Or the entire class can read the same book and choose characters from that book. You may want to provide specific guidelines for students. Here is an example:

Character Journal Guidelines

1. Think about the character you have chosen. Where does the character live? What does the character look like? How does the character dress? What is the character doing, thinking, and seeing?
2. Write each entry as you imagine the character would. Always include the date that the character would have used.

3. Write a journal entry for each chapter, commenting on the events of that chapter from the character's perspective.
4. Write your own personal thoughts after your entry. Use two colors: one for the character's thoughts and feelings, one for your own.

Double-Entry Journal. A double-entry journal is used for two separate entries that are related to each other. It provides a way to combine what one thinks and feels with what one is learning. Double-entry journals can be used for students to respond to various reading assignments or can be used to make writing an integral part of instruction:

For response to reading

1. Students divide a journal page into two columns.

2. In the left-hand column, they record details from the text, summaries, or quotations.

3. In the right-hand column, directly opposite the entries, they record their personal responses to what they read: observations, feelings, reactions, questions, or their own interpretations.

For instruction

1. Provide questions or directions that tap students' prior knowledge of the topic. Students record these in the left-hand column.

2. After instruction, students record what they learned from the lesson, including reading, listening, viewing, and discussing. These responses go in the right-hand column next to the relevant question or direction.

Here are some examples in different content areas:

Double-Entry Math Journal: In the left-hand column, students record a problem. In the right-hand column they write the process they used to solve the problem.

Double-Entry Science Journal: In the left-hand column, students write observations. In the right-hand column, they write questions, hypotheses, or conclusions about the observations.

Observations	Conclusions and Comments
The blue litmus paper turned red when we put it in the orange juice.	Orange juice contains an acid. That must be why they call it citric acid.

Reader Response Journal. A reader response journal is used by students to reflect on narrative fiction they are reading and to make connections between the story and their own lives.

1. Select a book with characters your students can relate to or identify with.

2. With students, plan a schedule for reading and writing. Post the schedule and make sure everyone adheres to it so that students will be reading the same parts of the narrative at the same times.

3. Use questions like these to stimulate students' thinking in preparation for writing:
   - How does the story make you feel?
   - Did this part remind you of anything you've experienced?
   - Who is your favorite (least favorite) character? Why?
   - What is your favorite part so far? Why?
   - What do you think will happen next? Why?
   - What has surprised you so far?
   - Does anyone in this story remind you of someone you know? Who? Why?
   - How is the main character like you?
   - How is the main character different from you?
   - Do you agree or disagree with what the main character did? Why?

4. Plan times for students to share and discuss what they have written in their response journals. Students can pair up or meet in groups of three or four to read and discuss their entries.

Learning Logs. Learning logs are for students to write about what they have learned, react to new learning and learning situations, record observations, raise questions, and perhaps identify problems they are having with learning. In the primary grades, students can start with drawing pictures and labeling them. Older students, who are more comfortable with writing, can still use pictures and diagrams but will probably use words for most of their entries. Here are some examples:

Math Logs. The use of logs in mathematics classes has become more and more prevalent, largely because students are being expected to explain the reasoning they used to solve a problem instead of simply doing the calculations. When writing in a math log students can use words, pictures, and numbers. Here are some examples of uses for Math Logs, each of which can be used as both a tool for learning and a means for assessing student's proficiency with the material:

- Write the problem, solve the problem, and explain the solution in writing.
- Define concepts and explain solutions clearly and logically.
- Develop diagrams, graphs, or charts that illustrate the concept learned or that show the process used to solve the problem.
- Reflect on learning:

  What I like most about math is . . .

  What I like least about math is . . .

  Today I learned that I . . .

  I was surprised that I . . .

  I noticed that . . .

  I discovered that . . .

Social Studies Logs. The use of logs in social studies can help students understand and retain the many details that they are learning in history, geography, economics, or other social science classes. Here are some examples of the uses for Social Studies Logs:

- Define important concepts in your own words. For example: in history—Manifest Destiny, imperialism, revolution; in geography—volcano, igneous rock, tundra; in economics—profit and loss, production, bonds.
- Construct time lines, charts, and pictures to keep track of important events in history, geographical areas, or economic systems.
- Reflect on learning:

  Today I learned that . . .

  I was most interested in . . .

  I am confused about . . .

  Learning about ___ made me think of ___ . . .

  I have these questions about ___ . . .

Additional Suggestions

- To encourage students to increase their fluency, have them count the words each time they write and keep track of their word counts. You may want to show them how to take an average of the number of words they write on one line of their journals so that instead of counting every word they can estimate the number of words by multiplying their average number of words per line by the number of lines. Students may even want to track their word counts over time so that they can see how they are doing. Such conscious attention to numbers of words written can motivate some students to write more.

- Some teachers use journals as a means of communication with students. In this kind of journal, usually called a dialogue journal, teachers and students hand the journal back and forth, commenting on one another's thoughts on almost any topic. For example, the teacher may invite students to write about their learning, reflecting on what they find difficult, easy, satisfying, or frustrating. The teacher then writes back, responding to whatever he or she wishes to comment on. Dialogue journals require a time commitment for both teacher and students, but they can be extremely satisfying. For students who do not usually enjoy writing, dialogue journals can be enjoyable because they have a clear and responsive audience.

- In conjunction with having students keep journals, you may want to have them read and discuss published journals of various sorts. For an example of a collection of journal entries by American pioneer women, see Hubalek (1995).

16

Key Word Notes

Overview and Background

Key Word Notes is a strategy for processing information while reading by writing and talking with a partner. The processing aids comprehension and retention, whereas the notes that are generated can be used in writing a summary of the information. The strategy is most appropriate and effective with informational material, although it can also be used when reading fiction or other works of literature.

This strategy was devised by one of the authors when advising a group of middle- and high-school teachers whose students were working on research reports. The teachers were concerned about students copying information directly from their references. They also suspected that the students did not fully understand what they were reading in the reference materials. The proposed solution came to be known as Key Word Notes. Although the strategy has been presented in handout form by the authors in workshops, this is the first time the strategy has been formally published. For more information about the principles of writing as a means of learning, on which this strategy is based, see Robinson (1993) and Marzano, Pickering, and Pollock (2001).

Instructional Benefits of This Strategy

- encourages attentive, active reading
- gives students practice in identifying important details
- provides opportunities for restating information
- encourages students to state and write information in their own words
- enhances retention of information after reading
- builds collaborative-learning skills
- gives students a study strategy they can use on their own

Step by Step

Before being successful with this strategy, students need experience identifying important details when they read informational text, and they need experience listening to and responding directly to a partner. When they are comfortable with these aspects of the process, here is how to proceed:

1. Have students prepare a page in their notebooks that looks like this:

   TOPIC: _____

1	2
3	4
5	

2. Divide the text students are about to read into four sections. Each section should be about 200–250 words long, which means it will probably include several paragraphs.

3. Have students write the topic at the top of their papers and note the beginning and end of the first section.

4. Organize students into pairs and give them the directions:

Read the first section to yourself and identify three or four words that you think will help you remember the most important information in that section. You may choose any words you like as long as you think they will help you remember the information. Write the words you choose in Box 1. When you and your partner have each chosen your words, take turns explaining what words you chose and what information they will help you remember. You may keep your books open as you talk and may refer to the text if you wish.

Limiting students to so few words keeps them from copying the text word for word. Also, because the task is to select words that will help them remember the information, they are more likely to think about the information as they read instead of reading quickly and inattentively.

5. When students have finished discussing their word choices for the first section, tell the class the ending point for the second section and have them read, select key words, write them in Box 2, and talk in pairs about their choices.

6. Repeat the process for the third and fourth sections of the text.

7. When students have finished reading all four sections, have them put the book aside and individually write about what they learned in Box 5, using all of their selected key words.

Here is an example of a reading selection about earthquakes and the beginning of a Key Word Notes page that one student created to help her remember what she read:

Feeling the ground move in an earthquake can be scary, but people are seldom hurt by the shaking. Instead, most injuries and deaths are caused by things that fall, break, or collapse when the earth moves. For example, windows may pop out of buildings and come crashing to the ground with great force. Brickwork in chimneys and on walls is easily weakened in a quake, and when the bricks pull away from one another and fall, they can injure people below. Large rocks on hillsides can also be dislodged in an earthquake and can tumble down onto houses, cars, and people without warning. Heavy tree limbs, too, may break off and fall, crushing property and injuring people.

Bridges, roads, and railway tracks can also be twisted and cracked in an earthquake. For instance, in the 1989 San Francisco quake, some highway overpasses buckled so badly that they had to be torn down. The roadway on one bridge gave way completely, leaving a gaping hole in the bridge high above the water of San Francisco Bay. Tunnels can also be dangerous places during an earthquake. No matter how well built a tunnel is, the walls may crack or collapse if the earth around it is jolted enough.

TOPIC: Earthquake Damage

1 not shaking break collapse	2 roads bridges tunnels dangerous
3	4
5	

Additional Suggestions

- At first, as students are learning the strategy, it's best to have them read short sections and choose only three or four words. As they become more adept with the process, you may wish to increase the length of the sections and also the number of key words students will select.

- If students do not catch on to the process, model for them by reading the sections with them, selecting your own key words, and sharing with the class which words you chose and why. You may also want to model how to write a summary of the information using all of the words you chose.

- You may wish to vary the number of sections, depending on the way the text is structured. For example, students might read only three sections before using their key words to write a summary, or they may read more than four sections.

- Encourage students to use this strategy on their own as they engage in research for reports or as they study content-area texts. They can pair up with a friend or they can simply pause periodically when they read, select words to help them remember the information, and summarize their learning in writing at the end.

17

Key Word Prediction

Overview and Background

This strategy is an effective way to prepare students for learning information from expository material. The teacher tells the students the topic, presents an array of words selected from the text, and invites discussion on how the terms might relate to the topic and to each other. Students form hypotheses, debate their ideas, and then peruse the material to confirm or refute their thinking. The material may be a content-area text, an audiotape, a film, or information from a Web site. After processing the information, they discuss what they have learned, returning to the key words to talk about how their thinking has changed and what they now know.

Stauffer (1969, 1975) introduced to teachers the Directed Reading-Thinking Activity, an approach to guided reading that involves speculation before reading. As he observed, when students speculate about what they might learn before reading, they exercise high-level thinking and become curious about the topic. Furthermore, because their hypotheses become their purposes for reading, they read attentively, motivated to seek answers. Following the tradition of Stauffer's DRTA, W. Dorsey Hammond invented the use of key words from the text as a stimulus for such thinking before reading (Hammond, 1984; Nessel, Jones, & Dixon, 1989). This variation on the original DRTA has been used since then in classes K–12 as a way to prepare students to read expository text purposefully and with motivation. For early discussions of the principles on which this strategy is based, along with recent commentaries and applications, see the following selected readings: Stauffer (1969, 1975); Hammond (1984); and Nessel, Jones, and Dixon (1989).

Instructional Benefits of This Strategy

- activates prior knowledge before reading, listening, or viewing
- arouses curiosity about the topic
- stimulates high-level speculation and prediction
- promotes student-to-student interaction
- encourages students to set purposes for learning

Step by Step

Before being successful with Key Word Prediction, students need experience forming hypotheses based on clues, listening to and responding directly to one another, and debating different points of view. When they are comfortable with these aspects of the process, here is how to proceed:

1. From the expository material, select eight to fifteen terms that relate to the topic and that can be associated with each other in different ways. You may use almost any words or phrases, including names of people and places, concrete objects or abstract concepts, and dates or other numbers. Choose words and phrases that you think students will probably know as individual words but that they will not readily relate to the topic. Such words will give them a base on which to generate hypotheses without knowing for sure if they are right. All the important concepts from the material do not need to be included because the purpose of the activity is to lead into the lesson and prepare students for comprehending the material, not provide a complete overview or teach unfamiliar vocabulary. Here are some examples.

    The first example is a set of terms selected by one third-grade teacher from a text that the students were going to read as part of a science lesson. The teacher introduced the lesson by saying: *All of these terms have something to do with kangaroos. You may not know what the connections are, but you can make some educated guesses. What do you think each one has to do with kangaroos?*

Kangaroos

8 months	250	12 to 15
20 feet	lima beans	joey
boomer	mob	tall grasses

Here is another example that was used by a sixth-grade mathematics teacher when beginning a unit on fractions. She knew the students had learned the terms in elementary school but had not worked with fractions recently. She wanted to see what knowledge they had retained while she piqued their curiosity as they began the unit. She introduced the activity by saying: *All of these terms have something to do with fractions. You have probably seen them before, but you may not remember what they have to do with fractions. What do you think the connections are?*

Fractions

numerator	whole	3/4
1/2	denominator	part
add	4/8	reduce
7/8	subtract	

Here is another example from a high school American History class that was beginning a unit on the War of 1812. The teacher focused on the writing of "The Star-Spangled Banner," an occasion associated with a critical event in that war, and introduced the lesson by saying: *All of these terms have something to do with "The Star-Spangled Banner," the national anthem of the United States. What do you think each one has to do with the anthem?*

"The Star-Spangled Banner"

Baltimore	Francis Scott Key	1779
British ship	1843	Ft. McHenry
newspaper	Washington, DC	prisoner
U.S. Attorney	lawyer	1931
William Beanes 1814	U.S. Congress	

2. Present the topic and the words, as illustrated in the examples above. Have students work in small groups to discuss how they think the terms relate to the topic and, possibly, to each other. Explain that the task is to form the best hypotheses they can. If students are hesitant, tell them to take the terms one at a time and decide what each may have to do with the topic, even if they need to guess. Encourage them by stressing that the quality of their thinking is more important than the accuracy of their responses.

3. Have the small groups share ideas as a whole class. Ask probing questions to encourage them to explain their reasoning. Ask them to listen carefully to each other, weigh the different perspectives that arise, and change their minds if they wish. Praise students for their thinking, but remain neutral about the accuracy of their statements so that they will not be overly concerned with guessing the right answers. Allow enough time for discussion so that students can thoughtfully weigh each other's ideas and consider the various terms from different perspectives. Here are some good questions and responses to use at this point to stimulate critical thinking:

   That's an interesting idea. Why do you make that connection?

   What do the rest of you think of that idea?

   That's one way of looking at it. Does anyone have another way?

   What leads you to think that might be true?

   Why do you say that? What train of thought led you to that point?

   (Student X) thinks ___. Do you all agree? Why or why not?

   (Student X) thinks ___. If that's true, what are the implications?

   Is there any other way of looking at this?

   What else might we have neglected to consider?

   (Student X) and (Student Y) seem to have very different perspectives. Listen to each side carefully and decide if you agree with one of them or have yet another idea.

4. When students have had time to debate their ideas and have become curious, have them turn to the material to get more information. When they are finished, they should return to the key words and talk about how they have revised their

thinking in light of what they have learned, citing evidence from the material to support their statements. They can discuss other information from the text, too.

5. For closure at the end of the lesson or unit, have students write or give orally a summary of what they have learned, using the original key words and any other important terms they want to include. At this point, the emphasis should clearly be on correct use of the words in the context of the topic.

Additional Suggestions

- If students are unfamiliar with this strategy, give them more support for the kind of thinking they need to do, being careful not to give away the correct information. For example, you might say: *What do you think lima beans have to do with kangaroos? Do you think kangaroos like to eat lima beans? Or do you think perhaps they damage lima bean plants by jumping on them? Or is there another possibility?* Such questioning should acknowledge initial thoughts while encouraging thoughtful speculation and critical evaluation of the ideas that are generated.

- Some students may try to approach the task by constructing a story that contains all the words because that is ordinarily easier than thinking about the relationships of the words to the topic. For example, they might say: *Once upon a time there was a kangaroo named Joey who loved lima beans. He weighed 250 pounds and was 20 feet tall when he was 8 months old.* And so on. Although this is one way to go about the task, it usually does not result in the kind of thoughtful reasoning that develops critical thinking skills while getting students ready to learn new information. In creating a story, the focus is simply on fitting all the words together into a narrative, however implausible or silly the result may be, and once the story is finished, its creators will be reluctant to rethink or revise. Such stories can be accepted on occasion, but students will think at higher levels if they are encouraged to focus on the connections the words have with the topic.

- Although it is usually best to use only words with which students are familiar, occasionally including an unfamiliar term or two can present an interesting and appropriate challenge. This variation is most effective if the term is important to the overall meaning of the passage and will serve to pique students' curiosity further. "Joey" is one such term in the array associated with kangaroos. Students unfamiliar with kangaroos are not likely to know this word, but they can still generate hypotheses about its connection to kangaroos, and when they see it in the text they will almost certainly have an "aha!" response that will make its actual meaning especially memorable.

- A variation for the primary grades is to select several words that are associated with the topic and a few that are not. Use words from the material students are about to read or hear and add a few that are not in the reading material and that have little to do with the topic. Give students packets of note cards with one word on each card, and have them sort the cards into "yes" and "no" piles according to whether or not they think the words have something to do with the topic. Or have one set of cards that you sort in front of the class as the students suggest different possibilities. This activity stimulates the same kind of thinking as the regular approach to Key Word Prediction but is somewhat easier in that students just need to make one decision for each word rather than deal with a variety of possible associations and combinations among the set of terms. Here's an example:

Topic: Snails

Directions   *Some of these words have something to do with snails*
(given orally): *and some do not. Sort them into two groups to show*
                what you think:

slime	shell
foot	nest
tongue	birds
frogs	feelers

(All the words except *frogs* and *nest* are in the picture book about snails that the teacher will read to the class.)

18

KWL

Overview and Background

KWL is a strategy for activating students' prior knowledge and organizing it for them to use as they read. Students identify what they know (K) and what they want to know (W) about a topic before a lesson or unit. After reading (or listening or viewing), they put what they have learned in writing (L). This strategy is used to guide students in their learning of subject matter, especially in elementary classrooms, and thus is best used with expository texts. KWL was modified to KWL Plus for secondary students with the addition of Mapping and Summarizing. After students complete several KWL Plus activities successfully, they can use the strategy for independent study.

KWL has been widely used in K–12 classrooms since its introduction and has been modified through the years in useful ways. For early discussions of the strategy as well as recent commentaries and applications, see the following selected readings: Ogle (1986a, 1986b), Carr and Ogle (1987), and Yopp and Yopp (1996).

Instructional Benefits of This Strategy

- activates prior knowledge
- provides practice in generating questions

- encourages students to read with clear purposes
- helps students identify misconceptions about a topic
- encourages students to think about resources and strategies for gathering information
- develops comprehension of the material
- provides a forum for reflection after reading
- keeps students actively involved in the lesson

Step by Step

You can use this strategy with the whole class to guide the reading of expository text material. When students are familiar with it, they can use it on their own in small groups or individually. Here are the steps to follow when working with the whole class.

1. Before introducing a new unit, theme, or topic, prepare a chart with three columns: K (What We Know), W (What We Want to Know), and L (What We Learned).

2. Introduce the new unit, theme, or topic. Display the KWL organizer on an overhead transparency or on a chart as a model, and organize students into small groups. Have each group create their own KWL organizer chart.

3. Ask students to brainstorm what they know about the topic in their groups. Have them put their ideas on strips of paper or note cards and put them in the first (K) column of their respective charts. For example, here are the responses of one small group of fourth graders who thought of what they knew about frogs at the start of a science unit.

K *What We Know*	W *What We Want to Know*	L *What We Learned*
Frogs live in water. They lay eggs. Young frogs are called tadpoles. Frogs eat insects. They can jump far.		

Encourage them to talk about where or how they got their information and, to challenge them to think critically, ask them to discuss how reliable they think their sources of information are.

4. Have each group look for ways to categorize the information in their brainstormed list, and encourage them to consider other categories that might also represent what they know. For example, here are the categories the same group of fourth graders generated:

K What We Know	W What We Want to Know	L What We Learned
WHERE THEY LIVE Frogs live in water.		
WHAT THEY DO They lay eggs. Frogs eat insects. They can jump far.		

WHAT THEY ARE
  CALLED
Young frogs are called
  tadpoles.		

5. You may want to consolidate the small groups' responses into a class chart or have the groups post their charts in the room.

6. Next, have students review what they know and discuss what they would like to know about the topic. Encourage them to note on their charts any gaps in knowledge, missing information, or conflicting information. Have them now generate questions, put them on strips of paper or cards, and add them to the second (W) column of their charts. Here are the questions the same group of fourth graders generated about frogs:

K _What We Know_	W _What We Want to Know_	L _What We Learned_
WHERE THEY LIVE Frogs live in water.	Can they also live on land?	
WHAT THEY DO They lay eggs. Frogs eat insects. They can jump far.	How many eggs do they lay at once? What kind of insects do they eat? Do they eat anything else? How far can they jump?	
WHAT THEY ARE CALLED Young frogs are called tadpoles.	When do you stop calling them tadpoles?	

7. Again, questions generated by groups can be consolidated onto one class chart or kept on the small-group charts. Leave the chart(s) posted as you go through the unit.

8. At the end of the unit, have students meet again in their groups to place revised and new understandings in the third (L) column and record any questions left unanswered along with any new questions they have. On the next page are some facts the fourth-grade group added to their chart after their first reading and the questions they had at this point.

In KWL Plus, use these additional steps:

9. Mapping. Have students organize the information they learned into categories, using their initial categories, new categories they think of as they learn, or both categories. Then have them record the information graphically, using a suitable graphic organizer. For example, they might place the title of the topic at the center of a concept map and have the categories extend from the center as branches, with details as "twigs" on each branch.

10. Summarizing. Have students use the map they have created as the basis for writing a summary of what they learned.

K	W	L
What We Know	*What We Want to Know*	*What We Learned*
WHERE THEY LIVE Frogs live in water.	Can they also live on land?	Tadpoles live in the water, and frogs live on land but also spend time in the water
WHAT THEY DO They lay eggs. Frogs eat insects. They can jump far.	How many eggs do they lay at once? What kind of insects do they eat? Do they eat anything else? How far can they jump?	The female lays hundreds of eggs. Tadpoles eat tiny water plants.
WHAT THEY ARE CALLED Young frogs are called tadpoles.	When do you stop calling them tadpoles?	Tadpoles turn into frogs in about 15 weeks, when they lose their tails and can breathe air with their lungs.
		How far can they jump? What kind of insects do they eat? How long do they live? How many kinds of frogs are there?

Additional Suggestions

- KWL is especially effective for students who are doing independent research with multiple sources of information. They discuss their prior knowledge and questions in small groups and as a whole class. Then they work individually, in partners, or in small groups to search for information using books, pamphlets, periodicals, CD-ROMs, online reference areas and bulletin boards, or people whom they interview. Individuals and groups then share the knowledge they obtained from different sources.

- Prepare blank KWL charts that students can use on their own. After modeling the strategy for students, have them use the charts in small groups as they follow KWL independently to read and study new material.

- KWL can be used to guide the reading of social studies, health, or science materials in several different lessons within a unit so that what students learn on one occasion will help them brainstorm what they already know on later occasions.

- When students are ready to write research reports, have them use KWL to guide their work, using the WHAT I LEARNED section as preliminary notes for the first draft of the report. KWL can also be used as a framework for completing I-Search reports. (See the discussion of I-Search reports in Chapter 12.)

- A variation of the KWL strategy is KWHL, the H representing *How We Are Going to Learn*. This fourth column encourages students to think about and list resources and strategies they can use to find answers to their questions.

- Another variation of the KWL strategy is the Smart Chart, which uses BKWL as the structure. The B represents the background information provided by the teacher before students begin their brainstorming. This is information that students may not have and clearly need to get started in discussing the topic.

19

List Group Label

Overview and Background

List Group Label is a strategy for stimulating inductive thinking about elements of a unit of study before beginning the unit. Starting with a list of terms related to the topic, learners organize the items into tentative categories, label the categories, and speculate about the identity of the topic. The strategy engages students in high-level thinking while preparing them to assimilate new information. As they categorize the details, they reveal their prior knowledge and have opportunities to evaluate their thinking critically. As they consider how the details may be related and what the topic might be, they become curious and motivated to learn.

Hilda Taba's interest in inductive thinking in the social sciences led her to create this strategy. Her constructivist approach to developing cognitive skills is aligned with earlier explorations by Jerome Bruner and others into the processes by which learners learn, organize, and retain information. These researchers recognized that instruction is particularly effective when students are encouraged to use what they know to generate tentative meanings that they can revise as they learn more. Such active involvement increases motivation to learn and, ultimately, comprehension of the material. For early discussions of the elements of the cognitive psychology underlying this strategy along with recent commentaries and applications, see the following selected readings: Bruner, Goodnow, and Austin (1956); Taba (1967); Taba, Durkin, Fraenkel, and NcNaughton (1971); and Joyce, Weil, and Calhoun (2000).

Instructional Benefits of This Strategy

- stimulates and develops inductive thinking abilities
- builds skill in categorizing
- activates students' prior knowledge and sets purposes for learning
- helps the teacher assess the quantity and quality of students' prior knowledge
- stimulates curiosity and increases motivation to learn
- develops critical thinking abilities

Step by Step

To be successful with List Group Label, students need experience with categorizing (sorting items and words into groups) and with inductive reasoning (making generalizations based on specific details). They should also be able to listen to and respond directly to one another in discussions. When they are comfortable with these skills, here are the steps to follow:

1. For the topic or concept that's the focus of the upcoming lesson or unit, identify a number of important content details, and put them on a list in random order. Try to keep the list to no more than 25–30 words so as to be manageable for the students. Make sure the words can be organized into several categories to encourage students to think flexibly. Here is one example of a list of details. Each word appeared in one or more selections that students were about to read in the course of the unit.

flowers	stinger	legs
honeycomb	hive	propolis
nectar	mouth	drones
honey	cells	guards
wings	brood	stomach
pollen	beeswax	antennae
legs	workers	queen
nest		

2. Write the words on small cards, one word per card, or arrange them, well-spaced, on a worksheet so that students can cut them apart and create cards for themselves. You will need one set of cards for each small group in the class.

3. Organize students into small groups and give each group one set of cards and several blank cards, or strips of paper, to use as labels. Give them directions like this:

> All these words have to do with what we will be studying next. With your partners, sort the words into groups (categories) to show how you think they go together. You should have at least two groups, but you may have more than that. When you have sorted all the words into groups, label the groups with a heading, using the blank cards. Last, look over your work and decide what you think we will be learning about. Put the topic on another blank card and place it above your labeled groups. This is an exercise in thinking and hypothesizing: you are not expected to know for sure how to group and label the words or what we will be studying; you are only expected to do your best thinking.

If there are many unusual words in the array, you may want to pronounce all the words for the students and have them say the words with you a few times so that they know how to pronounce them. You do not need to teach the meanings of the words, however, because students will learn meanings in the course of the unit. For this activity, unfamiliarity with meanings is acceptable and even desirable: not knowing will serve to arouse their curiosity and thus make the later learning more powerful.

Here is one possible set of groups and labels that a group might create with the list of words above:

TOPIC: Bees

Parts of a Bee	What Bees Eat	What Bees Make	Types of Bees
wings	flowers	beeswax	guards
legs	nectar	honey	queen
propolis	pollen	nest	drones
stinger		hive	workers
mouth		honeycomb	brood
cells			
stomach			
antennae			

4. When students have finished forming and labeling groups and speculating on the topic, have them share their thinking. You might have one or two groups put their ideas on the board or an overhead projector, or have the groups circulate around the room, noting each other's work and discussing how it is different from their own. As students articulate their thoughts, encourage them to evaluate their own thinking critically by asking questions like these:

    Why did you put ___ where it is? What's your reasoning?

    Are those the best groupings? Why?

    Are there other ways the words could be grouped or labeled?

    What are you sure of? Not sure of? Why?

    What questions do you have about the groupings others have made?

    Also encourage them to make any changes they may wish to make in their original groupings. Have students leave their cards where they are, or, if the cards need to be set aside, have students make note of their final groupings so they can refer to them later.

5. Now have students turn to the material to get more information. After reading, listening, or viewing, they should revise their original categories and labels to reflect what they learned. Here is an example of a revised array that shows what learning has occurred among the students who read about bees:

TOPIC: Bees

Parts of a Bee	Making Honey	A Bee House	Types of Bees
wings	flowers	beeswax	guards
legs	nectar	propolis	queen
stinger	pollen	nest	drones
mouth	honey	hive	workers
stomach		honeycomb	brood
antennae		cells	

Additional Suggestions

•   In the primary grades, List Group Label can be done with a set of large cards that are arranged on the board or in a pocket chart for the whole class to view and think about together. First, students discuss their ideas in small groups. Then representatives from different groups come to the front to show how they think the cards should be grouped and to tell why. The class as a whole then discusses what they think they are going to learn about. The activity can also be done as a review of material learned, in which case students will be recalling details and relationships instead of using them as a basis for inductive thinking.

- In the upper elementary grades and beyond, students can follow-up a List Group Label activity with writing. After they have revised their groupings and labels to reflect correct information, they put their reading materials away and write a summary of what they learned, using their groupings as notes and including as many of the terms as possible.

- In mathematics, List Group Label affords interesting opportunities for students to explore numerical patterns. For example, this list of expressions might be used for such an exploratory mathematics activity:

$3 + 4$	$67 \div 4$	$41 - 22$	$64 \div 8$
$8 - 5$	4×53	8×16	$297 - 156$
15×7	$43 + 59$	$112 + 42$	$87 + 91$
$40 \div 8$	$92 + 53$	$90 \div 5$	12×14
$29 + 8$	$79 \div 8$	$387 - 215$	$8 \div 2$
6×9	$25 + 72$	$63 - 5$	$49 - 7$
$15 \div 4$	$454 \div 4$	19×3	$38 + 62$
$60 \div 12$	17×5	$73 + 44$	30×3

The expressions may be grouped into categories in various ways. For example, they may be organized into four groups according to the operation represented (addition, subtraction, multiplication, division). They might also be grouped according to the answers that would result from doing the computations: for example, one-digit answers, two-digit answers, three-digit answers; or answers that are even numbers or odd numbers; or answers that are prime numbers or composite numbers. Other groupings are also possible. For example, one group of middle-school students put these expressions into two categories according to the answers: sequences of numbers that appear on a digital clock, and sequences that don't. Grouping and regrouping the expressions is an interesting and challenging way to build basic number sense while encouraging students to look for patterns.

For primary-grade students, the list may contain a variety of basic shapes or simple expressions such as $3 + 4, 4 + 4, 5 + 2, 5 + 3$, and so forth. For middle-school and high-school students, the list may contain any variety of mathematical terms, expressions, or symbols that students have learned or are about to learn or both.

- A variation of List Group Label is to present a topic to students, as a word or a picture or both, and have them brainstorm words that relate to the topic. Put the words on the board or on an overhead transparency, and have students work in small groups to sort the words and label the categories they create, adding items as they construct their groups. They can use their categorized words as a basis for writing. One such example is this initial list generated by a class of high-school students around the topic Our Favorite Things:

mystery stories	chat rooms	listening to music
charm bracelets	Friday night TV	old jeans
digital music player	soccer	TV cop shows
pepperoni pizza	old sci-fi movies	going to the cineplex
reading magazines	doing crosswords	video games
surfing	basketball	being with friends
parties with friends	popcorn	long novels
playing the piano	MP3 collection	making videos
being in a play	used bookstores	surfing the internet
pro football	playing the guitar	instant messaging
new jeans	rap	baseball
the coffee shop	hot chocolate	horror films

Students added items to the categories they generated, including such subcategories as individual song titles under a broad music category and many more examples of favorite foods and television programs. With the rich generation and discussion of ideas, each then wrote a composition on the topic, using whatever details they chose from the final array.

- A content-oriented variation involves giving students a broad topic connected to an upcoming unit of study and having them list, group, and label topic-related words that they already know. After students read, listen to, or view materials to get more information, they add to their categories, revising their original arrangements to reflect their learning. This activity can extend over the course of several days or, depending on the topic, can be an ongoing activity in a unit of instruction lasting weeks or months. Examples of topics in different content areas that might be used for this variation are as follows:

Social Sciences	Mathematics
government	measurement
important moments in history	geometric shapes
famous world leaders	computation
the stock market	patterns and sequences
Health and Physical Education	**The Arts**
anatomy	great artists
nutrition	types of music
basketball	types of dance
track and field	artistic media
Science	**Language Arts**
precipitation	novels
topographical features of Earth	mythology
chemical reactions	famous writers
circulatory system	characters in literature

20

Notetaking

Overview and Background

Notetaking while reading, listening, or viewing, is a strategy for recording and organizing important information in order to understand and remember it. Writing becomes a tool for learning, helping students comprehend information while generating an aid for later review and study. Stahl and colleagues (Stahl, King, & Henk, 1991) found that taking notes during lectures has a positive effect on the academic success of high-school students, and Marzano and colleagues (Marzano, Pickering, & Pollock, 2001) consider it one of the most effective classroom strategies for enhancing learning. When taking notes, students are engaged with the content in several ways. They take in information, make decisions, set priorities about what to record, write, and organize the information for later retrieval. Students need help to learn these important skills. Bakunas and Holley (2001) advise that strategies for taking notes should be taught explicitly just as other specific writing skills are taught.

Because there is no one right way to take notes in class, students can be taught several notetaking strategies and decide for themselves which method best helps them. Regardless of the approach used, a key to success is regular review and revision of notes (Pauk, 1974; Robinson, 1993). Regular review and synthesis of new information with previously summarized learning builds meaningful review into the process of learning a body of information.

Instructional Benefits of This Strategy

- enhances students' comprehension of instructional material
- encourages thinking about the topic
- generates an individualized study aid for students
- leads to improved retention of information
- provides students with a skill they can use independently in different classes and contexts outside of school

Step by Step

First, here are suggested steps for helping students use any approach to taking notes and use the notes as learning and study aids. Next are brief descriptions of four effective approaches to notetaking.

1. Model at least two approaches to notetaking.

2. Have students try each approach so that they become familiar with it and then discuss what they like about each one and which one they would like to use.

3. Have students focus on taking especially careful notes in one subject area for a week or two, using an approach they prefer. At the end of the time, have them bring all their notes to class and do one or more of the following activities to make active use of their notes. Model as needed to show them what to do.
   - With a partner, engage in Read Talk Write with your notes as the reading material. (Partners read their notes individually, put them aside, take turns talking about what they learned, and then write about the topic on new paper. See Chapter 24 for details about using this strategy.) Compare what you write with your original notes to see if you remembered all the important points.
   - Study a page of graphic-organizer notes, cover it up, and do your best to reproduce it from memory. Then check the original to see how much you remembered.
   - Review your notes for a week, then revise them so that the week's study is represented on only one page. That means condensing to retain only the most important points, combining graphics as much as possible, and so forth. (If students do this successively through a unit of study, they will benefit greatly from the reviewing and rethinking they'll do as they

repeatedly condense to one page. They keep all the original notes for reference as well as the one-page summaries.)

Here are four approaches to notetaking to model for students and guide them in using until they are familiar and comfortable with them.

Double-Entry Notes. Students draw a vertical line down the center of the page. On the left they record key pieces of information from the learning experience; on the right, they restate or summarize the information and add sketches or comments to help them remember it. For example, they might record definitions of math concepts on the left and examples of those concepts on the right. Or on the left they might write dates and key words for important events in history and on the right the connections they can make between those events and current events.

Notes as Graphics. Students keep their notes in the form of graphic organizers, arranging the ideas on the page in ways that make the relationships clear. (See Chapter 11, "Graphic Organizers," for details.) Some students like to use different colors to enhance the visual elements of their graphical notes still further (e.g., red for causes and effects, blue for a sequence of important dates, green for important names, etc.).

Main Idea/Detail Notes. Students draw a horizontal line near the top of the page. Above it they write a main idea from the material in their own words. Below it they write details that support that main idea. Students may decide to put two or three main idea/detail arrangements on a page, enclosing each one in a box to set it apart from the others.

Cornell System. This method was developed to help students at Cornell University improve their learning (Pauk, 1974) and is now the most widely used notetaking system in high schools and universities throughout the country. Students need a notebook with 8.5 x 11 lined paper. The page should be set up as shown in the illustration on the following page. Each page should be labeled with the date and numbered.

Here are the steps to follow to generate and use the Cornell Notes:

Record. Students record as many facts and ideas as they can in the right hand column during class.

2.5" wide Reduce notes to phrases or questions here.	6" wide Take notes here while listening or viewing.
2" high Recapitulate (summarize) all notes on this page here.	

Reduce or Question. After class, students read through the notes, reduce important information to key words, phrases, or questions, and write these in the column on the left. Doing so, students think about the information in a new way.

Recite. Students cover up the notes in the right-hand column, read each key word or question, then state aloud, in their own words, the information they recorded on the right.

Reflect. Students reflect on the material, making connections to prior knowledge and thinking about how they can apply the knowledge.

Review. Students review their notes nightly or several times during the week by repeating Step 3 (recite). This review increases the chance that they will retain the information.

Recapitulate. Students recapitulate or summarize the notes at the bottom of the page in the 2-inch block. The summary should be in each student's own words and should highlight the main points. Students should summarize each page of notes at the bottom of the page. Then they should summarize all the notes relating to a topic or unit on the last page.

Additional Suggestions

- Before giving students any instruction in notetaking, have them talk about their various approaches to taking notes when they read or listen in class. Then model one or more of the notetaking approaches described above, and have them choose one to use when they read the next chapter or listen in class for the next few days. Have students discuss how the instruction and practice have affected their notetaking behavior and their learning.

- Have students take notes regularly for several weeks or more with a partner, working with the partner to condense their notes to one page at the end of each week. Each member of the pair should make a copy of the collaborative one-page summary while retaining his or her original notes. Invite students to discuss with you what differences, if any, have occurred in their grasp of the material, in their retention of important ideas, and in the quality of their notes.

- Have students take notes individually on a lesson or unit, then meet in groups to compare their notes and create a new set of notes—as a group—that reflects all their understandings. Invite them to discuss the effect the collaborative review and notetaking have on their understanding.

21

Paraphrasing

Overview and Background

Paraphrasing involves putting material that someone else has said or written into your own words. In paraphrasing, one does not use the original wording or add one's own opinions. This form of speaking or writing is both a tool for learning and a means of monitoring or checking comprehension. It allows students to demonstrate their understanding while using their own language and style.

Giving students explicit instruction in paraphrasing helps them understand the difference between stating an idea in their own words and plagiarism. Several studies have found that even when students know they should not plagiarize, some not only do so but can give logical explanations as to why they do (Lewis, Wray, & Rospigliosi, 1994). Such findings indicate that paraphrasing is an important skill to teach students, especially if they must include information from text materials in reports.

Paraphrasing is also an excellent study technique because it requires students to process the information more thoroughly than when they state the exact wording of the text or copy the exact words into their notebooks. For more information about this critical strategy, see Robinson (1993), Lewis and colleagues (1994), Read (2001), and Duke and Bennett-Armistead (2003).

Instructional Benefits of This Strategy

- develops students' comprehension
- gives diagnostic information about students' comprehension
- allows students to monitor their own comprehension
- helps students incorporate material into their written work without plagiarizing

Step by Step

Students learn to paraphrase information by observing others doing it, by having explicit instruction in how to do it, by learning how to recognize when something is not in their own words, and by being expected to use their own words.

1. In preparation for teaching paraphrasing, try these activities, suggested by Duke and Bennett-Armistead (2003), to help students see that they can collect and report information without copying directly from a book or a Web site.
   - When beginning instruction in informational writing, have students write about something they know (a favorite sport, a special place) instead of researching a topic.
   - Have students consult resources that cannot be copied, such as viewing a video or interviewing someone.
   - Once students have gathered information have them use the Genre Exchange strategy (Lewis, et al., 1994). This strategy requires students to write the information in a form other than the original. For example, if the source is a newspaper article, the student might put the information into a poem or song.

2. To begin explicit instruction, have students read silently as you read aloud a paragraph from an expository text. Then paraphrase each sentence, using the board or an overhead projector, as they watch. Writing while they watch will help them see how to put information into different words while retaining the meaning.

3. Elicit suggestions from students about how to paraphrase another paragraph with you. Take a sentence or two at a time and record their restatements on the board. Model for them how to restate an idea if they have trouble breaking away from

the vocabulary and syntax of the original. For example, show them how they can start the sentence with different words, use synonyms for key terms, and use different sentence structures in expressing the ideas. When finished, read aloud the original and then the new paragraph to emphasize the differences.

4. Next, have students work in pairs to paraphrase short pieces of expository text—for example, a paragraph or two from a content-area textbook. Have groups share their work and discuss which paraphrased statements are especially good because the vocabulary and sentence structure are notably different from the original.

Additional Suggestions

- When you paraphrase your own statements in class, call attention to having done so. Such modeling will help students become more aware of how to say something in a different way. Here's an example:

    The primary food of bees is nectar that they collect from flowers. Here's another way to say that—a way to paraphrase it: Bees go from flower to flower gathering sweet juice called nectar, and that nectar is the main thing they eat.

- In discussions, ask students to restate instructional material and your own explanations regularly by saying *What does that actually mean? Say it in your own words.* If students can't explain something in their own words, chances are they don't understand it very well, so whenever they are asked to paraphrase, they will demonstrate their comprehension.

- Guide students to read, close the book, and restate the ideas in their own words when they are studying. This useful strategy is one step in such tried-and-true study methods as SQ3R (Survey, Question, Read, Recite, Review) and PQRST (Preview, Question, Read, Summarize, Test). It is also the basis of the Read Talk Write strategy presented in Chapter 24 of this book. Encourage students to monitor their comprehension when they're reading by pausing in this way to see if they can explain what they're reading.

- Have students read multiple books on one topic and engage them in discussions about what they have learned. Then, have them write what they learned without referring to the books.

- Focus on paraphrasing for a full week. Whenever students are discussing a reading assignment or are listening to an explanation, have them stop periodically to restate the information in their own words. Or have students write their restatements in their learning logs. Discuss with students what effect this has on their attention and comprehension.

22

Possible Sentences

Overview and Background

Possible Sentences is a prereading strategy that is appropriate for preparing students to read either narrative or expository material. Students are given several words from the material and are asked to create plausible sentences with them, which they then share and discuss with one another. The sentences are their predictions about how the words will be used in the selection they are about to read, predictions that they confirm or refute by reading. After reading, students think critically about the accuracy of their sentences in light of the material they read.

Possible Sentences helps students set a purpose for reading, motivates them by arousing their curiosity about the content of the reading material, and encourages them to think about the way the words might relate to each other. Students must draw upon their background of experience, their vocabulary, and their linguistic knowledge to generate sentences. Stahl and Kapinus (1991) found that this strategy improved students' vocabulary and comprehension of the material from which the words were selected. They noted that it was the discussion that made this strategy more effective than other vocabulary strategies, including semantic mapping.

Lenski and Ehlers-Zavala (2004) point out that English language learners benefit from experience with this strategy. They advise that these students should have heard most, if not all, of the words before and have a good idea about the word meanings so that they create plausible sentences. Through discussion, students learning English have an opportunity to use the words and gain meaningful repetition with various sentence patterns.

Possible Sentences can be used across all grade levels and in all content areas. For early discussions of the strategy as well as recent commentaries and applications, see the following selected readings: Moore and Moore (1986, 1992) and Tierney and Readence (2005).

Instructional Benefits of This Strategy

- activates prior knowledge before reading
- builds vocabulary
- encourages students to read with purpose and interest
- enhances comprehension of the material
- keeps students actively involved before, during, and after reading

Step by Step

1. Select several important words from the material that could be used in different ways in one or more sentences. Choose at least five or six words, including some that are probably new to the students and some that are probably familiar to them. Increase the number of words if students know the strategy and you want to give them a greater challenge. Display the words on the board along with the topic.

2. Tell students that all the words come from material they are about to read and that they are to create sentences that show how they think the author used the words in the material. Each sentence should contain at least two of the words in the display. Show them one or two examples, being sure not to give them sentences that actually appear in the text. For example, here are several words from a text about the manufacture of chocolate and two possible sentences the teacher might use to illustrate what students are to do:

Making Chocolate

picked	right	pods	beans
moment	flavor	roasted	ready
ripeness	fermented	time	temperature

Example 1: Chocolate comes from beans that grow in pods.

Example 2: The flavor of the chocolate depends on time and temperature.

3. Because collaborative efforts are likely to generate a greater number of sentences, organize students into pairs or small groups. Explain that they should aim for a variety of responses, even if some seem odd, that they should write as many sentences as they can, and that they need to use each word at least once in a sentence. Remind them that the name of the activity includes the word "possible" because the words can be used in sentences in several possible ways. You may want to have one student in each group act as the recorder for the group. This will facilitate sharing in the next step.

4. Have the groups share their sentences with the whole class. You may want to write as students dictate to you, or you may have students print their sentences on sheets of chart paper that can be posted for all to see. Underline or highlight the provided words in the possible sentences. Accept all responses without commenting on the quality of the sentences or the accuracy of the statements.

5. Have students read the material to find out how the author used the words and compare the author's sentences with their own. Here, for example, is part of the text about chocolate manufacture that contains the words used above in the example:

> Chocolate processing involves many steps. First, the beans must be picked at just the right moment of ripeness. Then they are taken out of their pods and fermented. (The fermentation develops the flavor.) Next, the beans are dried, and then they are ready for processing into chocolate. The dried cocoa beans are cleaned and then roasted. The length of roasting time and the temperature both affect the final taste of the chocolate.

6. After reading, have students return to their original sentences and critically evaluate them in light of the information in the text. They should have the text in front of them for reference as they engage in this discussion. In evaluating their sentences, they may choose to keep the sentence, cross the sentence out because it is completely inaccurate, or revise the sentence to make it a true statement. The focus at this point should be on the students' sentences, not on the sentences in the original. Students should use the text only as a resource in critically analyzing their sentences.

7. When students have finished evaluating their sentences, engage them in a discussion of any words that were new to them or that were used in a new way in the text. Give further explanations about the meaning of any words about which students are still uncertain.

8. Have students write new sentences, using the words from the original list and any other interesting words the class discussed after reading. They can return to their work groups to do this, or they can write sentences individually. This step can be used as a summative assessment of students' understanding of the material.

Additional Suggestions

- To vary the strategy, give students the list of words without the topic. Have them generate possible sentences and then predict what they will be reading about.

- Use Possible Sentences to introduce the reading of a work of literature, such as a short story. Include character names along with words that relate to the setting and plot. This strategy is also effective in priming students as they read a novel. Every chapter or two, give students a list of words that occur in the upcoming section of reading and engage them in Possible Sentences. The postreading evaluation of the students' original sentences will serve as a useful review of the story and as a discussion starter.

- When having students work on word problems, use Possible Sentences to prepare them for reading and solving the problem. Include numbers from the problem along with words. Here's an example:

Making Money

cars	$15.00	$4.00	buy
Marty	14	Brian	12
16	Tina	washed	earn

Examples of Possible Sentences:

Marty and Brian and Tina washed cars to earn money.

Tina washed 16 cars and Brian washed 12 cars.

Actual Problem:

Marty and Brian wanted to earn money and decided to wash cars on Saturdays. Tina, Marty's sister, said she would help. Their supplies cost a total of $15.00. They decided to charge $4.00 per car. Brian washed 16 cars, Tina washed 14 cars, and Marty washed 12 cars. How much was their profit?

23

Read and Think
Math (RAT Math)

Overview and Background

When students use Read and Think Math (RAT Math), they solve mathematical word problems by focusing on one part at a time, speculating on what the question will be and on what steps they will have to take to solve it. Debating their various ideas focuses their attention on the details in the problem and helps them relate to it as a real-life scenario. As a result, they learn to analyze problems more effectively and solve them with greater skill and accuracy.

The first step in George Polya's respected system for problem solving is to understand the problem. He also suggests thinking of similar problems, restating the problem, and devising a plan for solving it before beginning, all of which involve careful thinking and purposeful action. The close reading and careful reasoning used in a Directed Reading-Thinking Activity (DRTA), as described by Russell Stauffer, are similar to the kind of deliberate, purposeful thinking Polya advocates in mathematics. The RAT Math strategy builds on these traditions in mathematics and reading. The authors have presented it in teacher workshops and used it in mathematics classrooms for many years. For more information on the thinking underlying this strategy and on specific applications of it in the classroom, see the following selected readings: Polya (1945), Stauffer (1969), Dixon and Nessel (1992), and Nessel and Newbold (2003).

Instructional Benefits of This Strategy

- develops the habit of close reading
- encourages analysis of the scenario presented in the problem
- develops skill in making inferences
- encourages application of prior math knowledge
- raises interest in problem solving
- improves accuracy of computation

Step by Step

Before being successful with RAT Math, students need experience speculating, listening to and responding directly to one another, and debating different points of view. When they are comfortable with these aspects of the process, here is how to proceed:

1. Select a word problem with several sentences and the question positioned at the end. Separate the problem into three or four parts. Put the parts on an overhead transparency or on the board so that you can reveal them one at a time. For example:

> Some service dogs learn to obey 89 different commands. They learn these commands over the course of their training.
>
> Partner, a German shepherd, was taken to a 6-week training course and learned to respond to 14 commands a week.
>
> At the end of 5 weeks, how many commands did he still have to learn?

2. Organize the class into groups of three or four students.

3. Introduce the process to students by saying something like this:

> I'm going to show you a word problem one part at a time. You haven't seen this problem before, so you don't know what the question will be, but you can speculate. Discuss your ideas in your group and be prepared to share your thinking with the class.

4. Show the first part of the problem and have students discuss these questions within their groups:

> What do you think will be the question at the end?
>
> Why is that likely to be the question?
>
> What operations will you need to get the answer?
>
> What necessary information is still missing?

Explain to students that you don't expect them to know the actual question but that you are interested in their thinking.

5. After groups discuss their ideas for a few minutes, invite them to share their ideas as a whole class. Use the questions above to guide the discussion.

6. Show students the second part of the problem. Tell them they may find new information that will lead them to change their minds about the question. Have them again discuss in their groups and share ideas as a whole class. Use the suggested questions to guide the discussion.

7. Reveal the actual question and have students solve the problem.

The RAT Math process encourages students to read closely and process the information in the problem. As a result, they are likely to do a better job of actually solving the problem. Their speculations will arouse their curiosity, too, so that seeing the actual question will provoke an agreeable "aha" response. Regular practice with RAT Math will lead many students to internalize the process of pausing to think and understand when they are solving problems.

Additional Suggestions

- After finishing the problem, encourage groups to evaluate their initial hypotheses in order to decide which were the most reasonable in light of the information presented in the problem. Such critical thinking about their initial responses will help improve their thinking about subsequent problems.

- Have students solve any other interesting problems they might have generated in the course of speculating about the direction the problem was taking.

- When students have experience with RAT Math, you may want to have them conduct their own discussions in small groups. Provide each group with a problem, divided into parts, and appoint a facilitator to guide the discussion. To differentiate instruction, groups may be given different problems.

- Invite students to work in pairs or small groups to compose their own word problems and present them to the rest of the class using the RAT Math process.

24

Read Talk Write

Overview and Background

This strategy helps students learn to read carefully and put the information they've read into their own words. Students read individually, then pair up and take turns telling their partners what they read without looking back at the text. After partners have each had a chance to talk, they write (individually) what they learned. When students have regular practice with this strategy, they begin to internalize the process and use it on their own when they study, take notes for research papers, or want to improve their comprehension of almost any informational material.

This strategy was devised in the 1970s by a group of teachers and administrators, including one of the authors, who were collaborating to improve instruction in their schools and were concerned about the shallow comprehension they noticed in many students across grade levels. The students pronounced the words correctly and were able to read aloud fluently, but they were unable to remember and discuss much of what they read, even when asked to respond immediately after reading. Recognizing that students needed to talk, listen, and write as well as read, the educators worked out the protocol of Read Talk Write. The strategy had observably positive effects on students' comprehension and confidence as readers. Other benefits accrued as well: students enjoyed reading more and were better able to restate what they had read in their own words, all advantages when students were working on research reports as well as regular reading assignments. For more information about the strategy and about the talking-to-learn principles that underlie its efficacy, see the following selected readings: Britton (1970); Torbe and Medway (1981); Nessel, Jones, and Dixon (1989); Bomer (1995); Nystrand, Gamoran, Kachur, and Prendergast (1997); and Ketch (2005).

Instructional Benefits of This Strategy

- improves attention and concentration when reading
- improves comprehension of material read silently
- encourages students to monitor their comprehension while reading
- cements learning by having students restate ideas orally and in writing
- builds listening and speaking skills
- helps students learn to paraphrase information

Step by Step

Here is the basic Read Talk Write protocol. Information that can help make the process go smoothly follows these steps.

1. Organize students into pairs and designate one member of each pair A and the other B. If the class has an odd number of students, it's better for you or another adult to serve as a partner to a student than to set up a group of three.

2. All students start reading silently on your signal and read until you call time. Allow them 60 to 120 seconds to read.

3. On your signal, students stop reading and close their books.

4. One member of each pair engages in sustained (nonstop) talking about the material while the other listens, not replying or commenting. For example, all the designated A members of the pairs talk at once, addressing their respective partners. Talkers must do their best to keep talking, repeating what they said if they can't think of any new ideas. Listeners must listen attentively but may not say anything until it's their turn to talk. Allow 60 to 120 seconds for the talking. Books remain closed.

5. The other member of each pair takes a turn at sustained talking while the first talker listens without replying or commenting. The second talkers may repeat what their partners said if they can't think of anything new to say. Again allow 60 to 120 seconds for the talking. Books remain closed.

6. Students now write individually what they learned from reading, talking, and listening, still keeping their books closed. Allow as long for writing as you wish. When students have written as much as they can, they can reread the text to check details if they wish.

7. Repeat steps 1–6 two or three times, if desired.

8. After one or more rounds of Read Talk Write, you may wish to engage the whole class in a discussion of the material, have students write a final summary of what they learned, or in some other way provide closure.

For maximum success, explain the protocol fully at the start to make sure everyone understands what to do. Also, wait until after students have read to indicate who talks first so that everyone will prepare to be the first talker.

When the time for reading is up, indicate efficiently which member of each pair is to talk, perhaps by holding up a large A or B. Then give a brief, clear signal—for example, say "Talk!" or ring a bell. By saying as little as possible at this point, you will move students quickly from reading to talking and will not interfere with their ability to recall the information.

Ordinarily, two or three rounds of Read Talk Write are enough at one sitting. More than that may reduce the effectiveness of the strategy by introducing tedium. However, most students will benefit from having the whole class spend 10 or 15 minutes on the activity two or three times a week at first, then once a week thereafter. You may also wish to encourage students to use it with a partner when they're studying or taking notes for reports.

It's usually best, at first, to have everyone read the same text and start at the same place. Doing so allows for more effective talking and listening between pairs as well as meaningful whole-group reflection and discussion at the end. When students have more experience with the process, different pairs within the room can read different texts, and within some pairs the partners can read different texts.

Additional Suggestions

- After students have had some experience with Read Talk Write, have them share what they do while they are reading to help them remember information to talk about. Students may say they read some parts several times, try to remember key words, visualize details, rehearse what they are going to say, or use some other strategy to stay attentive and increase the chance they will remember the information when it is their turn to talk. Praise such strategies and urge students to try any they have not used before.

- You may wish to introduce drawing as a step between reading and talking (Read Draw Talk Write). Drawing a representation of meanings reinforces comprehension even more for many students and is enjoyable as well. This can be an especially useful variation for texts with information that can easily be pictured, such as a description of a person, a scene, or a process. Students each draw after reading, then tell their partners about their drawings when it's time to talk.

- In the primary grades, viewing may be substituted for reading, and drawing can be substituted for writing. For example, students may study a detailed poster or drawing, look away from the visual, and tell partners as much as they can remember about what they saw. Then they study the visual a second time, look away again, and again tell their partners what they recall seeing. Then individuals draw as much as they can remember of what they saw and talked about.

- In the primary grades, listening may be substituted for reading. For example, you may read part of a story or account to students and then pause for partners to tell each other as much as they can remember about what they heard. After several rounds of listening and talking, the final activity can be drawing or writing a summary of the information or story.

- When students are tackling word problems in math classes, Read Talk Write can become Read Talk Compute or Read Draw Talk Compute. Students work in pairs to silently read a word problem, close the book, take turns talking about the details of the problem and what they might do to solve it, check back to make sure they remembered the details correctly, and then solve the problem either individually or collaboratively. Pausing to talk things over with a partner before starting to solve the problem can help many students concentrate on what is being asked.

25

Readers' Theater

Overview and Background

Readers' Theater involves students performing a play that they have created themselves from a nondramatic text. The material used as the foundation may be a short story, part of a novel, a scene from a biography or autobiography, or nonfiction material from science or social studies texts or articles from periodicals. For example, fictional and historical accounts of the American War for Independence, the War Between the States, the women's suffrage and civil rights movements, and current-affairs accounts in periodicals are among the many texts that can be used in a social studies class as a basis for Readers' Theater activities.

Readers' Theater has a positive effect on students' thinking and learning because the translation from one mode of discourse to another is a cognitively challenging, yet enjoyable, task. Students must make decisions about the characters to include and the scenes to portray and must also decide how to convey important information in actions, dialogue, and narration. Even when the original material is simple and straightforward, students benefit by the thinking that goes into these decisions. The strategy is also appropriate for English language learners, who benefit because it incorporates listening, speaking, reading, and writing in an authentic context (Lengling, 1995). For early discussions of the value of such scriptwriting, and other aspects of classroom dramatization, see Moffett (1968, 1973).

Readers' Theater gives students the chance to take on the attributes of the characters in their play, thereby gaining a deeper appreciation and understanding of them and of the events of the play (Young & Vardell, 1993). Because Readers' Theater involves repeated readings during rehearsals, students become more fluent and confident readers (Rasinski, 2000). Such practice is useful for all students and is especially beneficial to students who need extra support in reading or language learning. Finally, the experience of reading aloud or performing a drama helps students understand the importance of appropriate expression to convey meaning (Barone & Morrow, 2003).

Instructional Benefits of This Strategy

- develops oral reading and oral expression skills
- deepens comprehension of the original text
- integrates reading, writing, listening, and speaking
- highlights the differences between drama and other forms of discourse
- brings a text to life and makes it more personally meaningful

Step by Step

To create a play with students, guide and model at first, inviting them to chime in with ideas. After they have written two or three plays this way with your help, they will be ready to proceed on their own.

1. Choose a text that is familiar to the students and that lends itself to dramatization. Reread the text with students and think aloud about where to break it into sections. Lead students to see why some places make better breaking points than others (e.g., because they involve major turning points). Explain that these sections will become acts in the play.

2. Reread each section again with students to review the action and note which characters are involved. Also, decide if narration might be needed for effective transitions between scenes. Some Readers' Theater plays do not need a narrator, but the role is useful for handling transitions when dialogue alone cannot provide enough information.

3. Work out with students the sequence of events within each act, noting which characters are involved and what the content of the conversation between them needs to be. A storyboard of

the sequence is helpful at this stage. The storyboard should contain simple sketches to indicate who is in each scene and notes to indicate what is happening.

4. Using the text and the storyboard as guides, write the dialogue, any narrator's statements that might be needed, and directions for the readers. This is the heart of the process and can involve considerable thinking and careful interpretation of the original text. In collaborating with you on this step, students will see that descriptions and information given in stories often need to be conveyed in dialogue.

As an example, here is part of the text of a folktale from the Brothers Grimm, retold here, and a play script that was written from it.

The Bremen Town Musicians

Once upon a time, a donkey grew so old and tired that his master decided it was time to get rid of him. The donkey sensed this and before the master could lead him to slaughter, he ran away, following the road to Bremen. As he trotted along, he thought to himself that once he got to town he would look for work as a musician.

Before long he came upon a hound who was lying, exhausted, by the side of the road. "What's wrong, my friend?" asked the donkey.

"Poor me!" said the dog. "Because I can no longer hunt, my master was going to put me to sleep. I saved my life by running away, but what will I do now?" . . . .

The Bremen Town Musicians: A Play

Narrator: After many years of carrying heavy loads, a donkey overheard his master saying it was time to get rid of him. So he ran away. As our story opens, the donkey is on the road to Bremen, a town far from his master's farm.

Donkey: Hee-haw! Hee-haw! I can't believe my master was going to send me to the slaughterhouse! It is a good thing I escaped. I don't know what I'll do when I get to Bremen, but I think I'd like to try being a musician. Anything but carrying heavy loads on my back! (*Pause*) Oh my! That dog up ahead looks like he's in trouble!

(Continued)

(Continued)

Dog:	Ohhh! Ohhhh!
Donkey:	Hello there, Dog. You sound very upset. What's the matter?
Dog:	I served my master faithfully for many years, but when I grew too old to hunt with him, he told his wife he was going to have me put to sleep. I saved my life by running away, but what will I do now?

5. Continue working back and forth between the original text and the script until you and your students have completed a first draft. Add director's notes to describe the actions of characters, their facial expressions, and scene details.

6. Have students assume roles and read the draft aloud to see how it sounds and to make sure the important points of the story are all included. Revise as needed.

7. Prepare a final version and make copies for the students. Have them practice reading the play aloud several times until they're ready to perform for an audience. Students do not need to memorize the script, but they do need time to rehearse so that they read (or recite) fluently and with expression. There is no need for elaborate costumes or staging; simple props, such as paper hats or cardboard objects, will do. You may wish to have different groups of students perform the play on successive occasions. Each new group of performers is likely to bring its own interpretations to the lines and actions.

8. After students perform, hold a class discussion about the success of the play, what everyone learned in the process, and whether they will change anything the next time they are engaged in Readers' Theater.

Additional Suggestions

- Use the process of developing the Readers' Theater script as a writing assignment. Have students describe the technique for preparing the script, directing the characters, reading aloud, and performing for an audience. Students might also prepare a list of tips for putting on a successful Readers' Theater play. The audience for the assignment might be another class that has not yet had experience with Readers' Theater.

- Combine an author study with Readers' Theater. For example, if you have engaged students in an author study on Patricia Polacco, students will know that she uses many of the characters over and over again in her stories: her friends, her brother, her father, and her grandmother. When students read several of Polacco's books, they will develop a deep understanding of the characters, including their manners of speech and their typical actions. This will help them portray these characters in Readers' Theater plays.

- For a longer text, use a modification of the Jigsaw strategy as described in Chapter 14 of this book. Divide the text into segments and have each group turn their segment into a play. Allow groups to meet and compare scripts before combining into one long script. Each group can perform their own script, or they can exchange scripts and perform each other's.

- Extend the Readers' Theater experience by having students respond to questions regarding actions or choices made by the characters by writing in a character's voice.

26

Reciprocal Teaching

Overview and Background

Reciprocal Teaching (Palincsar & Brown, 1984) involves students and teacher sharing the responsibility for leading the conversation around a reading selection or other learning material. Ordinarily, the conversations include four reading strategies: predicting, clarifying, summarizing, and questioning. At first, the teacher models how to lead the conversation, thinking aloud to show students how to respond to the text; then students reciprocate by taking the lead. Practicing in small, cooperative groups, students assume more and more responsibility to question, summarize, clarify, and predict while reading and discussing. As students become more independent, the teacher continues to monitor and evaluate their participation to determine what additional support they may need to refine their skills.

Students' comprehension increases when using Reciprocal Teaching for several reasons. When they generate questions, they take ownership of the reading process, no longer relying on the teacher or the author to question them. They learn that reading is an interaction between themselves and the text. When they seek clarification, they learn how to monitor their own comprehension and recognize when they are not sure of the meaning of what they are reading. They also learn the importance of rereading, using text aids, and seeking clarity in other ways. When they summarize, they identify the important points in the text and integrate this content with what they already know. When they predict, they use text information to think ahead, rather than just recalling the information. Because students work in cooperative groups to address these four purposes, they rely on each other to help them comprehend. Brown, Palincsar, and Purcell (1986) conclude that the strength of Reciprocal Teaching is that it focuses on reading to learn rather than learning to read.

Research has shown that regular use of Reciprocal Teaching increases students' comprehension, improves the quality of their dialogue, and increases their skill at writing summaries while also improving their participation in class and decreasing behavior problems (Palincsar & Brown, 1984, 1986). Others have found that students improved their reading skills almost immediately when they began using the strategy (Allen, 2003; Palincsar & Klenk, 1991). Palincsar and Klenk (1991) reported improved results when using a series of content-area texts related by theme or concepts, such as the animal survival themes of adaptation and extinction.

For additional discussions of the strategy, see the following selected readings: Palincsar and Brown (1985); Brown and colleagues (1986); Lysynchuk, Pressley, and Vye (1990); Palincsar and Klenk (1992); Brown and Campione (1992); and van Garderen (2004).

Instructional Benefits of This Strategy

- helps students actively comprehend
- provides opportunities for students to learn to monitor their own learning and thinking
- gives students opportunities to practice reading strategies with real text
- scaffolds instruction
- enables peers to support each other's learning
- encourages all students to participate
- fosters relationships between students of different abilities

Step by Step

Begin by teaching and modeling all four comprehension strategies separately: predicting, questioning, clarifying, and summarizing. Students will be able to engage in Reciprocal Teaching more easily if they are practiced in their use of each strategy first. They also need to understand that skilled readers use all four of the strategies regularly and in conjunction with each other while reading.

Reciprocal Teaching is a very social activity; students collaborate as they construct meaning and gradually assume the role of the teacher. The use of small, heterogeneous groups ensures that each student has adequate opportunities to practice the four reading strategies while receiving feedback from peers and from you. Frequent, guided practice with this structured interaction is essential. Many students will need 15–20 sessions or more to begin to feel comfortable with the process and to learn to collaborate productively.

The four strategies can be used in any order, but they should be used during the reading. That is, students should pause periodically to clarify, summarize, question, and predict rather than read all the text material first and use the four reading strategies at the end. Here is a suggested sequence to follow to get students started:

1. Select a content area passage that can be divided into two or three parts.

2. Have the students read the first section of the passage silently. Ask a few questions about the information in the passage and have students respond. Vary the kinds of thinking involved in answering the questions, focusing on high-level thinking as much as possible. For example, ask one or two questions that require recall of information that is explicitly stated in the text; one or two questions that require inferential thinking, drawing conclusions, or another such cognitive activity; and one or two questions that model how a good reader queries the text. The point of the questioning step is for the reader to maintain an active, inquiring mind about the information while moving through the text.

3. Summarize the passage by restating the most important points. Explain how you decided on what to include in your summary, for example, by pointing out that you omitted several details in favor of stating a main idea.

4. Point out one or two elements in the passage that at first impeded your comprehension, such as unknown words, unclear referents, complicated syntax, or confusing organization. Verbalize how you clarified these elements. For example, explain how you reread a part, checked the glossary for a word meaning, or looked at an illustration.

5. Predict what you think you will read next, pointing out in the passage the clues on which you based your predictions.

6. Continue to the next sections of the passage and repeat steps 2–5, again modeling the four strategies. In this second modeling, you may wish to invite students to chime in with their own questions, summary statements, elements that they clarified, and predictions. Model for students in this way several times, each time encouraging them to participate more and giving them feedback to help them improve their skill at using the four strategies. Then have students practice Reciprocal Teaching on their own in small groups of 4–6.

Here are examples of prompts you may wish to use with students as you model and guide their practice with the four strategies:

Reading Strategy	
Questioning	One question I had when I read was . . . ? From this bit of information, I wonder if I can infer that . . . ? Is the author implying . . . ? Is ___ (information in the text) comparable to ___ (something known from past experience)? I wonder . . . ? Who . . . ? What . . . ? Where . . . ? When . . . ? How . . . ? Why . . . ?
Clarifying	One of the words I wasn't sure about was . . . What other words do I know that I can use in place of . . . ? What words or ideas do I need to clarify? This is confusing me. I need to _____ (identify the strategy) to figure this out.
Predicting	After thinking about what I just read, I think I will next be reading about . . . (with expository text) Based on what has happened so far, this is what I think will happen next. . . . (with narrative text) I'll probably find out more about . . . Based on what I know about this character, I predict that he/she will respond by . . .

Summarizing	What does the author probably want me to remember from this information? What are the most important points in what I just read? What would the teacher ask about the main idea? In my own words, this is about . . . The main idea is . . .

Additional Suggestions

- If you are using a difficult text, combine Reciprocal Teaching with the Jigsaw strategy. First, assign each student group a paragraph or two rather than the entire chapter. After they have used Reciprocal Teaching to understand their section, form new groups with members who have read each of the assigned sections, and have them share what they have learned. (See Chapter 14 in this book for information on the Jigsaw strategy.)

- While students are working in groups, walk around the room listening in and writing down questions, predictions, elements to clarify, and important points that should be included in the summary. Then lead a whole-class debriefing of the content and the process.

- Organize students into groups of four. Assign each student a role: Predictor, Questioner, Clarifier, Summarizer. Have students read and take notes, then discuss the text from the point of view of their role. Students can switch roles and repeat the process as they continue with the next segment of text.

- Use a modified version of Reciprocal Teaching to help improve students' comprehension of word problems in mathematics. The components of this version are clarifying, questioning, summarizing, and planning (van Garderen, 2004). One student, the designated group leader, takes on the role of the teacher. After reading the word problem, the group clarifies any words or phrases they do not understood. Then the group leader uses questions to help the group identify the key parts of the problem. Next, the leader, with input from the group, summarizes the problem and restates the question. The group then creates a plan for solving the problem. As other problems are tackled, each person in the group takes a turn being the leader.

27

Saturation Reporting

Overview and Background

A saturation report, also known as a sensory report or an eyewitness report, is an original piece of reporting based on the student's close observations of an occasion or a place. To create such an account, students take in sights and sounds and other sensory impressions, saturating themselves with the experience and taking notes on the spot. Then they select and organize their impressions into a composition that brings the experience alive for readers while conveying their own perspective on the occasion or place.

Saturation Reporting is based on research into sensory writing undertaken by James Moffett (1973). This kind of writing brings greater authenticity to composition assignments in that it allows students to use their firsthand experiences as a basis for their writing and encourages them to articulate their own impressions and perspectives on their chosen topic. What they write thus comes directly from what they know and what they choose to share with an audience. For early discussions of the strategy along with recent commentaries and applications, see the following selected readings: Moffett (1973, 1992), Duke (1981), and Strong (2005).

Instructional Benefits of This Strategy

- stimulates interesting, original writing
- develops observation and reporting skills
- connects writing directly to students' own lives and experiences
- refines and extends general writing abilities
- prepares students for writing other kinds of reports that are based on information obtained from interviews, books, or sources other than firsthand experience

Step by Step

Here are the steps to take in helping students write a saturation report. You will probably want to allow several days or more to complete the sequence.

1. Decide on the places or occasions in school or in the community that would be suitable for saturation reports, or have students brainstorm ideas with you. In-school assignments are effective for all students but are especially good for younger children; older students might go farther afield during the school day, with parental permission and teacher supervision, or go to locations outside of school as the basis for their reports. Here are a few suggestions for places that can yield good experiences for this assignment:

In the School	Outside the School
cafeteria during lunch	hospital emergency room
library or media center	grocery store or other retail
lobby or main office	shop
playground	public library reading room
main hallway	restaurant or snack bar
school assembly	museum or public park
school sports event	parade or other celebration
science fair	public sports event
physical education class	live concert
	school board meeting

2. Assign a place or occasion to each student. Several individuals, or the whole class, can be given the same assignment, if desired. Explain the purpose of the writing. You may also want

to put the directions in writing so that students can refer to them when they are "in the field" as reporters:

Name _____   Assignment _____

You've been given a plum assignment, Reporter!

Go to your assigned place and observe carefully.

Write down interesting sights, sounds, and smells. Make note of details of the surroundings as well as what people are wearing, doing, and saying. Jot down words and phrases, and draw sketches. Take it all in!

Think about the overall impression the place makes on you so that you can convey that in your report.

---

3. Back in class, have students look over their notes and decide on the general impression their respective places or occasions conveyed to them. For example, a school cafeteria might convey an impression of noisy exuberance and camaraderie, whereas a public library reading room might have an atmosphere of studious concentration. Think of the general impression as the focus of the report—the main idea or thesis that the details will support. Talking at this point can be very helpful in deciding on the general impression and can help students formulate the ideas they will use in their reports. Organize students into pairs or small groups and have them tell each other about what they experienced, reflect on their impressions, and add any details to their notes. Then have them compose first drafts. Depending on the students' age, writing experience, and your own expectations, a draft may be as short as a paragraph or as long as several pages.

4. Have students meet in small groups to respond to each other's drafts, helping each other sharpen the focus, choose better words, rearrange details for maximum effect, and in other ways make revisions to the content of their compositions. Next, students can work with partners to edit their revisions to refine spelling, punctuation, and other mechanical elements.

5. Publish the saturation reports in some way. Collect them in a notebook for display in the school media center, circulate them to other classes, or post them in the hall. Keep copies to use as examples for the next round of reports or for students in another class.

Additional Suggestions

- Bring in and have students bring in examples of sensory-rich writing from books and periodicals. Display these in the classroom, or collect them into a notebook or file, for easy reference when students are planning and revising their compositions. Call attention to specific features of the examples. Point out how one writer uses a string of interesting adjectives to describe a scene and another makes effective use of dialogue. Encourage students to use the same features in their own writing.

- Give pairs of students the same assignment so that they can work together to observe, take notes, and generate a report collaboratively. Two-person reports are especially suitable for students who are less-experienced writers, although experienced writers can also learn a great deal by collaborating with a peer. Students may write more and write better when they work in pairs.

- Encourage students to return to the same places on different occasions, each time composing a new saturation report. The several reports can be compiled and published in a booklet.

- Plan to have students complete four or five saturation reports during the school year. At the end of the year, have them select their favorites for inclusion in a published memory book that everyone can have as a keepsake.

- Encourage students to present their reports as multimedia presentations, supplementing the writing with photos, drawings, or video footage. Some students may be interested in transforming an eyewitness report into a film documentary.

- When students have learned the basics of Saturation Reporting they can use their skills to gather and analyze information in a variety of places to supplement their learning in specific content areas. For such assignments, students can go to the places on their own (after school or on weekends), or the whole class might go together. You may want to get permission in advance from those in charge to make sure they have no objections to student "reporters" collecting information on their premises. Here are some examples:

- As part of a consumer math unit, have students go to a retail store and position themselves near the entrance. While noting details and impressions, have them also count the number of people who enter the store in a given period of time. After they've written their report, have them solve such problems as these:

> Given the number of customers you counted, how many people do you think visit the store in a day? A week? A month? A year? What if customers, on average, spend $50 ($25, $100, etc.) each time they visit the store? How much money would the store take in per day (week, month, etc.)? How representative was the time you spent at the entrance? Was it busy, slow, or somewhere in between? How does that judgment affect your conclusions about sales?

- As part of a science unit, have students go outside to observe and report on trees, flowering plants, animals, and other aspects of the natural world. For instance, in one school, the teachers planned an extensive interdisciplinary unit focusing on a large nearby river. They used class visits to the river, followed by saturation reports, as a kickoff activity and returned with students periodically for more and more detailed observations along the riverbank as they studied the history of settlements along the river and the effect of an ever-growing population along the present-day river.

- As part of a health unit, have students go to a variety of restaurants to observe the overall ambiance and to note specifically the kinds of food that customers order. Have students estimate or get from the manager nutritional information on the menu items. In their reports, have them describe the experience of being in the restaurant and also write about the nutritional qualities of the food consumed.

- Have students visit an art museum to gather details about the works on display, the visitors who went through when they were there, and the overall feel of the place. In addition, have students interview a few visitors to get their reactions to the exhibit and to art in general. Students might do similar reports based on visits to a concert or a theatrical presentation.

- As part of a local history unit, have students visit different places that have historical significance in the area and write saturation reports on their impressions. Then have them gather historical information and compare the early days of the place with the place as they observed it.

28

Scrambled Words and Sentences

Overview and Background

This strategy involves mixing up words or sentences so that students can put them back in order. Teachers at all grade levels have used out-of-order language for this purpose for many years. The game-like features of these activities appeal to students, whereas teachers appreciate how they develop language and cognitive skills. When reordering words into a sentence, students must think about what sounds right syntactically and what makes sense semantically. If they discover more than one arrangement, they can evaluate the effectiveness of the different possibilities or discuss any changes in meaning that may result from a changed sequence. When reordering sentences into paragraphs, students must think about the order of ideas and must use transition words, referents, and other textual clues in making their decisions.

Scrambled Words is popular with primary-grade teachers and teachers of English to nonnative speakers because of the opportunities the strategy affords for students to explore and master sentence patterns. Scrambled Sentences (sometimes called Strip Story) can effectively deepen the comprehension and challenge the thinking of older students, including, for example, students at a university law school, as described in one of the sources below. For early discussions of these scrambled-language strategies as well as recent commentaries and applications, see the following selected readings: Moffett (1973), Nessel and Jones (1981), Dixon and Nessel (1983), and Heath (1994).

Instructional Benefits of This Strategy

- develops awareness and understanding of word and language patterns
- provides opportunities for logical thinking about the order of words in a sentence or of sentences in a paragraph
- promotes active involvement in reading
- deepens comprehension

Step by Step (Scrambled Words)

1. To prepare for a Scrambled Words activity, compose or select three or four sentences at an appropriate level of complexity, that is, neither too simple nor too complex for the students who will be working with them. For most students in the primary grades and for many English language learners, short simple sentences with highly familiar words will be the best choices. For example:

   The dog ran down the street.

   My sister and I sat in the car.

   The bird flew high above our heads.

   For most older students, longer and more complex sentence structures will provide the right level of challenge. For example:

   When the rain began to fall, the spectators opened their umbrellas.

   Despite her fear of heights, Samantha agreed to take a ride on the roller coaster.

   The whole class left the room at the same time and went to the library together.

2. Print the words clearly on small cards, one word per card, and put the cards for each sentence into a small envelope. (A 3 x 5 note card will yield 6 or 8 cards of the right size.) If students will be working in pairs or groups, prepare several sentences for each pair or group.

3. Give the envelopes to the students and tell them to arrange the cards in each envelope into a sentence that makes sense. Encourage students to work together, discussing their thoughts and reading their various attempts aloud to see how they sound. You may want to model for them how to do this if they are not sure how to proceed.

4. Have students share their final arrangements by reading them aloud to the whole class. They may come up with different arrangements, each of which can be considered correct. Encourage them to discuss why they made the decisions they did.

5. Show them the intact sentences, written on a chart or a transparency. Have them read the sentences with you in unison, or read them aloud to model effective language.

Step by Step (Scrambled Sentences)

1. To prepare for a Scrambled Sentences activity, choose sentences from a paragraph that students can read comfortably. The number of sentences will depend on the age of the students and their experience with the strategy. With younger or more inexperienced students, you may use only four or five sentences; with older or more experienced students, you may use as many as 15 sentences. Here, for example, is a set of sentences from one paragraph that was used with a middle-school class:

Scrambled Sentences: An Example

The average person couldn't afford to drink chocolate, though.
In fact, the first European chocolate factory was not built until 1728.
It was only many years later that chocolate became more common.
Then Christopher Columbus imported cocoa beans from North America to Spain in 1502.
It was too expensive.
After that, chocolate became a favored drink among the wealthy people of Europe.
Long before people in Europe heard of chocolate, the Aztecs in Mexico were making a drink from cocoa, honey, and maize.

The original order is as follows:

> Long before people in Europe heard of chocolate, the Aztecs in Mexico were making a drink from cocoa, honey, and maize. Then Christopher Columbus imported cocoa beans from North America to Spain in 1502. After that, chocolate became a favored drink among the wealthy people of Europe. The average person couldn't afford to drink chocolate, though. It was too expensive. It was only many years later that chocolate became more common. In fact, the first European chocolate factory was not built until 1728.

2. Put the sentences on paper, leaving plenty of space between them so that they can be cut apart. It's usually best to put the sentences in random order on the page so that the irregularities in the cutting can't be used as clues to the correct order. Put each set of cut-up sentences in an envelope.

3. Distribute the envelopes to pairs or small groups of students and tell them to arrange the sentences so that they make sense as a paragraph. Encourage students to work together, discussing their thoughts and reading the sentences aloud as they work. You may want to model for them how to do this if they are not sure how to proceed. Encourage them to attend to clues such as transition words and referents.

4. Have students share their final arrangements. You might have students walk from one work station to another to see how others ordered the sentences, or you might have students post their arrangements in the same area on the board so that all can see any differences in the arrangements. They may come up with different arrangements, each of which can be considered correct. Encourage students to discuss why they ordered the sentences as they did and to debate the effectiveness of different arrangements.

5. You may also want to show them the intact paragraph and have them read it in their groups or with you as a whole class. Most students will be interested to see how close they came to the order of the original.

Additional Suggestions

• To make Scrambled Words more challenging, write all the words in lowercase so that students have to put more thought into identifying the first word of the original sentence. Give them small slips of paper on which to print the capital letter of the word they decide is the first and superimpose it on the lowercase letter.

- To use Scrambled Words as an exercise in punctuation as well as word order, include the marks of punctuation on separate cards so that students will need to decide where to place the punctuation as they order the words.

- Scramble words or sentences from different kinds of text material, including narration, exposition, poetry, and drama. Have students discuss which texts are the most challenging to put in the right order and why.

- In mathematics, use Scrambled Sentences with story problems. The effort students exert to figure out the order of the sentences will result in closer attention to the information contained in the problem.

- Use Scrambled Sentences with the first paragraph of a text as a prereading activity. Figuring out the order of the sentences in the first paragraph can arouse students' interest and curiosity while giving them practice with some of the words in the material.

- Have students rewrite their own paragraphs as a list of sentences to cut up and exchange with other students. This exercise gives students new perspectives on their writing. For example, one student may have difficulty figuring out the original order of sentences in a peer's paragraph because the relationships among the sentences are not clear. Students can discover more effective ways of organizing their sentences because of what their peers do with their original paragraphs.

29

Think-Pair-Share

Overview and Background

Think-Pair-Share is a strategy for getting students to respond more frequently in class and to stay actively involved by interacting with each other as well as the teacher. The teacher poses a question or gives a prompt, then directs students to

- *Think* (individually) about your response
- *Pair* with another student and discuss your ideas
- *Share* your thinking with the rest of the class

The teacher allows a few minutes for each step, then moves students to the next step with a signal. Some teachers use hand signals whereas others use a small bell or other audio signal. When students are experienced with the routine, they can do it on their own when they're working in small groups. This effective strategy can be used in grades K–12 in all content areas to help students process information, think more deeply about it, and communicate their thoughts and responses.

First developed by Frank Lyman at the University of Maryland, Think-Pair-Share has been used extensively in the field of cooperative learning. By allowing students time to think, the strategy has been shown to improve students' responses to questions (Stahl, 1990).

More recently, Think-Pair-Share has been used in content area classes to help English language learners (ELL) process and comprehend difficult text (Zainuddin, Yahya, Morales-Jones, & Ariza, 2002). Think-Pair-Share gives ELL students the chance to formulate their own ideas, try them out in a nonthreatening way with a partner, and then share them with the class. For early discussions of the strategy as well as recent commentaries and applications, see the following selected readings: Lyman (1981), McTighe and Lyman (1988), Stahl (1990), Kagan (1994), and Zainuddin and colleagues (2002).

Instructional Benefits of This Strategy

- increases time on task and active involvement
- provides time for students to formulate and "rehearse" their responses before offering them to the whole class
- fosters positive interdependence, giving students opportunities to learn from one another
- encourages students to listen to each other
- provides a change of pace from the usual interaction pattern, in which the teacher talks, one student talks, and the teacher talks again

---

Step by Step

1. Explain the steps, making sure students understand the purpose of each. As a reminder, you may want to post a brief explanation. Here's an example:

   > THINK-PAIR-SHARE
   >
   > **THINK**: Concentrate on the question, think about possible responses, and decide what to say.
   >
   > **PAIR**: Discuss your ideas with a partner and listen to your partner's ideas.
   >
   > **SHARE**: Tell your ideas to the whole class when it is your turn.

2. Decide on the signal you'll use to indicate the start of each step. For instance, one ring of a small bell could mean *think*;

two rings could mean *pair*; three rings could mean *time to share*. If you want to use hand signals, try two fingers touching the head for *think*, crossed fingers or clasped hands for *pair*, and a hand extended outward, palm up, for *share*. Practice the signals with students until they are all familiar with them.

3. Practice Think-Pair-Share at least once every day when you're conducting whole-class activities. Some occasions when students might use the strategy are
   - when responding to a reading assignment
   - during a hands-on activity
   - when discussing a film or other visual presentation
   - as a prewriting activity for generating ideas

Additional Suggestions

- In math class, present a problem to the whole group. Have students solve the problem on their own individually. Then have students pair up to talk to each other about their solutions, comparing notes about how they went about solving the problem as well as the answers they obtained. Finally, have several students share their solutions with the whole class.

- In science class, use Think-Pair-Share when students are getting ready to conduct experiments. After giving the assignment, first have students think through the steps of the experiment individually. Then have students pair up, tell each other the steps they would use, and agree on what they will need to do. Then several students can share with the class what steps they will follow.

- Use Think-(Write)-Pair-Share as a variation. Have students write down their answers before talking with a partner and sharing with the whole class. Think-(Write)-Pair-Share can be used with both literary selections and informational textbooks in various subject areas. In preparation for the activity, determine stopping points for discussion and record these on the board or on a handout. Have students read to the stopping points and record their thoughts individually. Then have them pair up to share their thoughts. Then, several pairs can share their thoughts with the whole class. Repeat the steps until students have read the whole selection.

- Add a step, so that the strategy becomes Think-Pair-Four-Share. In the added step, two pairs discuss their thoughts before sharing with the whole class. Assign one person in the foursome to be the reporter after the two pairs have discussed their ideas. This variation gives students additional opportunities to formulate and share their ideas in a nonthreatening context before speaking to the whole class.

30

Writing Frames

Overview and Background

Frames for writing have only structural elements that serve as a guide for students' own writing. Such frames provide students with templates that allow them to organize their thoughts in logical, written form. They contain key words or phrases, such as leads, transition words (first, second, then), and other elements that help students organize their thoughts and writing. Frames help scaffold students' writing and can be used in conjunction with either narrative or expository compositions.

When teaching writing using a frame, the type of writing is first introduced with the critical elements highlighted. The frame is then presented, and students and teacher fill in the frame with their own ideas. Students then use the frame to write individually. As students gain confidence in their own writing and learn the structure of the particular kind of writing (i.e., narrative, expository) the use of frames is discontinued. Many teachers start with a paragraph frame and then move to a frame with multiple paragraphs for a three- to five-paragraph piece.

Teaching writing with frames helps students of all ages and all abilities. The strategy has been used with students from kindergarten through high school. Teachers find frames particularly useful with students who need help in understanding a particular kind of writing, students who find writing difficult, and students who have special needs in literacy. Recent research has shown that the use of writing frames is beneficial for English language learners because of the structure and language support. Teachers have noted that after only one or two uses of a frame, students begin to internalize the structure and language features of the frame so that their writing becomes more coherent and fluent. For early discussions of the strategy as well as recent commentaries and applications, see the following selected readings: Nichols (1980); Lewis and Wray (1995); Dahl and Farnan (1998); Rothstein and Lauber (2000); Marzano, Pickering, and Pollock (2001); and Woods and Harmon (2001).

Instructional Benefits of This Strategy

- provides a model for organizing and writing paragraphs
- provides structural prompts linked to a particular writing genre
- provides appropriate language structures for different writing tasks
- helps students develop and expand their own paragraphs
- highlights the different organizational structures of paragraphs
- enables students to internalize patterns for expressing their ideas

Step by Step

You'll want to model this strategy first and then complete a writing frame with your students before having students use it on their own. First, introduce the type of writing students will be learning. Next, present a writing frame for one paragraph on an overhead transparency or on the board, and add ideas or information to show students how to build up the paragraph. After one or more such demonstration sessions, use these steps next:

1. Give students the same frame that you modeled and have them create their own paragraphs using it. For example,

My Favorite Television Show

My favorite television show is _____. I like the show for several reasons. First, _____. Second, _____. Third, _____. Those are the reasons I think _____ is such a great program.

2. Have students present their paragraphs, explaining why they used the ideas they wrote.

3. Give students a different frame based on the same organizational pattern as the first. For instance, after giving students the frame shown above, try one like this to give them more practice with this pattern:

Opinion Frame

I am very much in favor of _____. Here are my reasons for having this opinion. First, _____. Next, _____. Finally, _____. Those are the reasons I am in favor of _____.

---

4. Have students share their paragraphs so they can see how the same frame can be transformed into a variety of different paragraphs.

5. Have students work with other frames that are based on different organizational patterns. For instance, if you've focused on opinions supported by reasons, you may want to have students work next with chronological order, comparison or contrast, or cause-effect patterns.

6. Once students are comfortable with writing one paragraph, expand their writing to multiple paragraphs. For example, you can use the following frames for a two-paragraph comparison-contrast piece.

Comparison-Contrast Frame

_____ and _____ have many things in common but are also different. They both have _____. They are similar in that _____. They both resemble _____.

_____ and _____ are different in some ways. For example, _____. In addition, _____. Another difference is that _____.

---

7. After a round of practice, post examples of completed paragraphs in the room for students to refer to when they write without the use of frames.

Additional Suggestions

- Use Writing Frames for helping students write out the process they use in problem solving. Present a problem and have the class solve the problem and work with you to write what they did, using the frame as a guide. Then present a new problem, divide the class into small groups, and have each group solve the problem and write what they did, using the frame. Once the groups have finished, have them present their paragraphs and compare them.

- Introduce a frame paragraph of any organizational pattern you want to focus on. After students have written one or more paragraphs with the frame as a guide, have them skim periodicals for examples of other writers' paragraphs that follow the same kind of pattern and compare them with their own.

- Find a paragraph in a newspaper or magazine that illustrates good adherence to a pattern of organization. Prepare a frame from that paragraph for students to use as a guide. When they've written their own paragraphs, have them compare theirs with the original.

- Have students write a persuasive piece using the following frame:

Argument Frame

Although not everyone thinks the way I do, I want to argue that . . .

I have several reasons for thinking this. My first is that . . .

Another reason is . . .

Also, . . .

Furthermore, . . .

Therefore, although some people think that . . .

I think I have explained why . . .

- Have students write a piece that explains how to do a task that involves several steps. Collect their first drafts and put them aside. Next, introduce a frame with a chronological-order pattern and have students use it in writing an explanation of a different multi-step task. Then return students' first piece to them and have them revise in light of what they learned from using the chronological frame as a writing guide. You may wish to use this frame:

> **How to Frame**
>
> To _____, you will need _____.
> First, _____.
> Next, _____.
> Finally, _____.

- Focus on writing frame activities for a week or more. Then have students return to writing without these aids. Have students compare their writings and see if they notice any differences in the quality of their writing before and after the time spent using frames.

Resource

Combining Strategies: Sample Lessons

Each of the strategies in this book can be used at different grade levels and in different content areas to enhance student learning, but they can also be combined to increase their effectiveness. For example, students can respond to an Anticipation Guide before reading an informational text to activate their thinking and set purposes for reading. Then they can use the Jigsaw to develop their comprehension of the information as they read. Finally, they can use a Graphic Organizer after reading to represent the information they learned. Such a combination of strategies keeps students purposefully involved in thinking and learning throughout a unit of instruction.

This chapter contains eight sample lessons to illustrate strategy combinations that result in elevated thinking and achievement. Here is a summary of the eight.

Sample Lesson	Grade	Content Area: Topic	Strategies
Lesson #1	1	Science and Language Arts: Ladybugs	Key Word Prediction Listen Draw Talk Write Paraphrasing Scrambled Sentences
Lesson #2	3	Science: Growing Potatoes	Possible Sentences Jigsaw Read Draw Talk Write
Lesson #3	5	Language Arts: Character Study	Frayer Model DRTA (Narrative Text) Facts and Inferences Character Journals Reader's Theater Imitation Writing

Sample Lesson	Grade	Content Area: Topic	Strategies
Lesson #4	6	Mathematics: Measurement of Areas	RAT Math Read Draw Talk Write Graphic Organizer Learning Logs
Lesson #5	8	American History: The Pony Express	Anticipation Guide Readers' Theater Cubing
Lesson #6	9	Mathematics: Circles and Angles	DRTA (Expository Text) Think Pair Share Read Talk Write Learning Logs
Lesson #7	10	World History: Alexander the Great	List Group Label Carousel Key Word Notes Graphic Organizer
Lesson #8	11	Language Arts: Descriptive Writing	Saturation Reporting Freewriting Think Pair Share Cloze Procedure Analogies

Each example follows a similar approach: strategies are combined so as to engage students before, during, and after reading, listening, or viewing. The emphasis is on high-level thinking and high-level comprehension of the curriculum material, and each involves a certain amount of collaboration among pairs or small groups to complete tasks and discuss ideas.

The combination of strategies used at one grade level can easily be used at another with curriculum topics and materials suitable for that level. For example, Key Word Prediction, used here in a sample first-grade lesson, also leads to engaging and enjoyable discussions in secondary classrooms, whereas Saturation Reporting, used here in a sample high-school English lesson, leads to lively writing in second grade as well. It is hoped that these examples, though designated for specific grades and content areas, will spark ideas for the design of lessons at other grades and in other content areas.

Sample Lesson #1

Subject: Science and Language Arts

Grade Level: Grade 1

Topic: Ladybugs

Purposes:

- Orient students to the topic and assess their existing knowledge
- Engage students in hypothesizing so as to develop these thinking skills while also piquing their curiosity
- Engage students in collaborative thinking so as to maintain their attention and interest while also allowing them to pool their knowledge and skills
- Help students learn to listen to each other and respond to one another's ideas
- Give students specific purposes for listening and speaking
- Build reading vocabulary

Strategies:

Key Word Prediction

Listen Draw Talk Write

Paraphrasing

Scrambled Sentences

1. Students worked in pairs or groups of three to sort words into two groups: words that have something to do with ladybugs, and words that do not, in a variation on Key Word Prediction. Each group had one set of these words on note cards.

six legs	snakes
wings	case
black spots	aphids
spiders	eggs
honey	leaves

2. After a few minutes of collaborative discussion and sorting, the teacher asked different groups to share how they had arranged their

words. As the students explained, the teacher showed the arrangements they described, using a large set of the same cards and YES/NO category headings. The teacher asked students to share their reasoning and expected them to listen to each other and tell if they agreed or disagreed with each other and why.

3. The teacher then read aloud a picture book about ladybugs, stopping at strategic points to ask students if they had heard any of the words they had been discussing. If students missed hearing a word, the teacher reread the page to give them another chance. As students acknowledged having heard a word, the teacher pointed to that large word card on the board and, if necessary, moved it to the YES column. The teacher also asked students to state in their own words what the word had to do with ladybugs, reinforcing the concept of paraphrasing that the class has been working on. For example:

Teacher (reading):	The larva is growing into a ladybug. It has six tiny legs that will grow as the larva becomes an adult ladybug. Did you hear any of our words?
Students:	Six legs!
Teacher:	Who can tell the group what you learned in your own words?
Student:	The book says that the babies have six legs, and they still have six legs when they get to be big.

By stopping periodically to have students note the key words and paraphrase important information, the teacher helped students develop their comprehension of the factual material.

4. After finishing the book, the teacher asked students to draw a picture of something they had learned about ladybugs. Students shared their pictures by holding them up and stating briefly what they had learned that they had represented in their pictures. This gave them another opportunity to paraphrase the information in the book and to listen purposefully to one another.

5. Next, the teacher had students work again with their collaborative partners on a Scrambled Sentences activity, using simple sentences about ladybugs that included some of the words they had been discussing along with some of the high-frequency words they were

learning. Each student received a page with sentences that the teacher had prepared, a partial example of which is shown here. Students cut out the words, mixed them up, and arranged them into sentences on their desktops. The teacher included the numbers so that students would know which words went together in each sentence:

1	1	1	1	1	
The	ladybug	has	six	legs	
2	2	2	2	2	2
Ladybugs	have	wings	and	black	spots
3	3	3			
Ladybugs	eat	aphids			

Students worked individually on their sentences, but they were encouraged to work together and to read aloud the sentences they composed. They then put the word cards into envelopes so that they could do the activity again several times in the next few days.

Sample Lesson #2

Subject: Science

Grade Level: Grade 3

Topic: Growing Potatoes

Purposes:

- Orient students to the topic and assess their existing knowledge
- Engage students in hypothesizing so as to strengthen these thinking skills while also piquing their curiosity
- Keep students actively involved in learning by having them use linguistic and nonlinguistic forms of expression
- Engage students in collaborative thinking so as to maintain their attention and interest while also allowing them to pool their knowledge and skills

Strategies:

Possible Sentences

Jigsaw

Read Draw Talk Write

1. Students worked in Jigsaw home groups to arrange words from the text into possible sentences. Here are the words they were given and the text from which they were taken. Each group was asked to write at least four sentences, using at least two words from the array in each sentence:

lumps	part	water	fork	leaves
potato	ground	dig	hairs	sunlight

Growing Potatoes

(1) You can grow a potato plant by planting part of a potato in the ground. A thin shoot starts to grow up from the potato piece, and roots start to form, too. The new plant uses the piece of potato as food for a while. As the plant grows, it needs water and more food. The roots

---

spread out under the ground to take in water and food. They are covered with tiny hairs that draw in the water and nutrients from the soil. The shoot pushes up above the ground and forms a stem and leaves. The leaves soak up sunlight.

(2) A growing potato plant can't use all the food it takes in from the soil, so as it gets bigger, it starts to grow small lumps in the ground near the roots. These lumps, called tubers, store extra food. They grow larger as the plant grows. These tubers are the parts of the plant we eat. When the tubers are growing, they need to stay under the soil so that no sunlight reaches them.

(3) If a tuber gets uncovered and light reaches it, the skin will turn green where the light hits it. The green parts on the skin are poisonous, so you should cut them away when you are fixing potatoes to eat.

As a potato plant grows, buds form on the stems near the leaves, and soon flowers are blooming. In the middle of each bloom there is a fine powder called pollen. Insects visit the plant to eat the pollen, and while they're eating it, they get some of it on their bodies. The pollen sticks to their bodies when they fly to another potato flower. When the pollen rubs off on the next flower it fertilizes the flower, and fruit will grow from that spot. Potato fruits are small, green balls with tiny seeds inside. They are poisonous. If you plant one of these seeds in the ground, a potato plant may grow, but it's usually easier to grow a new plant from a piece of an old potato.

(4) People harvest potatoes by digging them up with a special large fork. Next, the potatoes have to be washed. After the tubers are clean, they can be fixed in lots of different ways. They can be baked or fried or boiled or steamed over boiling water. You can also put potatoes in soups or make potato salad, and some people even make potato bread. Besides being tasty, potatoes also help you stay healthy because they have lots of minerals and vitamins, especially calcium, potassium, and vitamin C. The best way to eat potatoes is to boil them or bake them. If you fry them in oil, the added fat makes them less healthful.

2. Students read their possible sentences aloud in their home groups, and then each group chose the three they liked the best to read aloud to the whole class. The teacher engaged students in a discussion of why they wrote the sentences they did, inviting them to share what they thought they knew about growing potatoes.

3. The teacher reorganized the students into Jigsaw expert groups and gave each group one of the four parts of the passage to read and discuss. (Some groups were given the same passage because there were more than four groups in the class.) The expert groups read their passages, discussed the information, and decided as a group how to illustrate the information in one or more pictures. Students talked about the information as they worked on their pictures, and though each individual's drawing was somewhat different, each contained the essential information the students had decided they needed to share.

4. The teacher moved the students back into their home groups, which now contained at least one person from each of the expert groups. Students used their drawings as teaching aids when they shared what they learned in their home groups.

5. When all the information was shared in the home groups, individuals wrote or drew a summary of all that they had learned and then engaged in a final whole-class discussion of what they had learned.

Sample Lesson #3

Subject: Language Arts

Grade Level: Grade 5

Topic: Character Study

Purposes:

- Orient students to the topic and develop the concept of honesty
- Engage students in making inferences about character from story details
- Give students opportunities to respond personally to the story
- Challenge students to convert the story into a different form
- Help students improve their sentence fluency, using models of effective writing from the story

Strategies:

Frayer Model

DRTA

Facts and Inferences

Character Journals

Readers' Theater

Imitation Writing

1. The class was about to read "The Indian Cinderella" as part of an extended instructional unit that involved comparing and contrasting different versions of this classic folktale.[1] In this Native American version, the "prince," named Strong Wind, can make himself invisible and has other amazing powers. His sister is his companion and assistant. The Cinderella character, who is unnamed in this version, wins his favor because she tells the truth when the sister challenges her with a series of questions. The learning activities that followed took place over the course of several days.

---

1. Many variations of "Cinderella" exist across cultures. The version used in this lesson was from Clarkson and Cross (1984).

2. Before reading, students used the Frayer Model to explore the concept of honesty. First, they worked in small groups to generate examples and non-examples of honesty and to talk about the essential and non-essential characteristics of honest behavior in their own lives, in stories they had read, and in movies or television programs they had seen. Groups shared their thinking, and the teacher consolidated the ideas into a class chart.

3. Next, the class read the folktale. They followed the procedures of the DRTA, stopping twice to predict outcomes, first in small groups and then as a class. During the whole-class discussion, the teacher asked questions that encouraged the students to focus on the characters' attributes. For example: *Why do you think that character might do that? What have you learned so far about the character that leads you to make that prediction?*

4. After students finished the story, they returned to their Frayer Model chart and continued their discussion about honesty, adding to the chart and refining their understanding of this concept in light of their reading of the folktale.

5. Next, students worked in pairs to generate inferences about the characters in the story, using the Facts and Inferences strategy. At the teacher's direction, they concentrated on inferences they could make about the attributes of the various characters in the story. For example, they inferred that Cinderella showed patience at several points in the story and honesty at the end, that the other young women were impatient, mean, and dishonest, and that Strong Wind and his sister were comparable to a god and goddess. Their discussions during the DRTA prepared them for this closer analysis of the characters' attributes.

6. Students were then given a choice of one of four characters from the story: Cinderella, one of her sisters, Cinderella's father, or Strong Wind. They wrote two Character Journal entries from their chosen character's point of view: one for a day before Cinderella met Strong Wind and one for a day after they married and continued Strong Wind's work together. Students shared their writings in small groups by reading them aloud.

7. Next, students worked in groups of four or five to write scripts for plays based on the story. Each group had the choice of retelling the whole story in their play or of concentrating on one or two important

scenes. They were to make sure their scripts reflected the character study in which they had been engaged during the DRTA and the journal writing. Students needed two days to work on their scripts and rehearse their plays; then they performed them for the whole class. The preceding work on character analysis was put to use in this Readers' Theater activity.

8. For writing practice, students engaged in Imitation Writing, using the following sentences from the story as models:

> On the shores of a wide bay on the Atlantic coast there dwelt in old times a great Indian warrior.

> There lived in the village a great chief who had three daughters.

Sample Lesson #4

Subject: Mathematics

Grade Level: Grade 6

Topic: Measurement

Purposes:

- Help students understand specific mathematics concepts
- Develop students' ability to comprehend a mathematics word problem
- Help students learn to explain the reasoning behind their solution
- Engage students in collaborative thinking so as to maintain their attention and interest while also allowing them to pool their knowledge and skills

Strategies:

RAT Math

Read Draw Talk Write

Graphic Organizer

Learning Logs

1. To help students improve their skill with problem solving, the teacher organized students into small groups and engaged them in RAT Math with this problem, divided into three parts as shown:

> Lucas and his brother, Con, want to decorate their room with posters. Their parents agree that they can put posters on two walls of their room. Each wall is 10 feet high and 12 feet long.
>
> The posters they want to put up are 30 inches wide and 36 inches long.
>
> How many posters will they be able to put up altogether?

2. Once students had seen the question, they worked in their groups to continue talking about the problem and to draw a representation of the two walls and the posters, referring to the details of the problem. (This was a variation on Read Talk Write.) The groups then used their

drawings as aids in working on a solution to the problem, which they did collaboratively.

3. Each group shared its solution with the rest of the class, using their drawing to explain their reasoning. The teacher facilitated the discussion, encouraging students to listen to each other and to question each other's thinking and procedures. Through this process, students achieved consensus as to what the correct answer had to be.

4. Each small group then used a Graphic Organizer, in this case a flowchart, to represent the steps they went through in solving the problem.

5. Individuals then wrote in their Math Learning Logs an explanation of how the group had solved the problem, using the group flowchart as their notes.

Sample Lesson #5

Subject: American History

Grade Level: Grade 8

Topic: The Pony Express

Purposes:

- Orient students to the topic and assess their related knowledge
- Engage students in hypothesizing to strengthen these thinking skills while piquing their curiosity to learn about the topic
- Engage students in collaborative thinking so as to maintain their attention and interest while also allowing them to pool their knowledge and skills
- Keep students actively involved in learning through the use of engaging, thought-provoking activities

Strategies:

Anticipation Guide

Readers' Theater

Cubing

1. Before reading, the teacher gave students a brief explanation of what the Pony Express was so that they all had a small amount of information on which to base hypotheses. She said:

> Many years ago, the Pony Express was organized as a way of delivering mail as quickly as possible from one part of the country to another. Men carried the mail on horseback, riding as fast as they could until the horse needed rest. Then they would stop at a rest station, jump on a new horse, and keep riding until they needed rest. Then they would hand the mail off to a new rider who would continue. The handoffs continued in this way until the mail reached its final destination.

Then students worked in small groups on an anticipation guide, using the teacher-provided information and their reasoning skills. The groups then shared their thinking with the whole class and debated their ideas. These are the statements that were used and the text on which they were based.

Anticipation Guide: The Pony Express

___ 1. When heading west, Pony Express riders began in Chicago, Illinois.
___ 2. Riders changed horses about every 15 miles.
___ 3. Pony Express riders earned about $100 a week.
___ 4. To send a one-ounce letter by Pony Express cost $10.
___ 5. The Pony Express was in operation for about 10 years.

The Pony Express

During the 1850s, mail was usually carried across the U.S. by stagecoach. It took about 25 days for the stage to go from Missouri to California, using a southwesterly route through El Paso and Tucson that the Postmaster General considered safe and sure for year-round travel. Then William Gwin (senator from California) and William Russell (owner of a freight company) set up a faster system of mail delivery—the Pony Express. These men were angered by the choice of a southern route, believed that a central route was feasible, and wanted to prove it. In organizing a better system, Russell also hoped to win a government contract for delivering the mail.

Pony Express mail service began on April 3, 1860, starting in St. Joseph, Missouri. From there, the riders followed the Oregon Trail through Nebraska and Wyoming and then headed south to Salt Lake City. Then they rode west across the mountains through Carson City, Nevada, ending the run in Sacramento, California. From Sacramento, the mail went by steamer to San Francisco.

Ads for Pony Express riders asked for young men, preferably orphans, who were eager for adventure. The work was hard and dangerous. Day and night, in all seasons, the men had to ride through the wilderness, sometimes chased by hostile Indians, to carry the mail. Riders earned from $100 to $150 a month, which was very good pay in those days.

Riders changed horses at relay stations, which were set up about every fifteen miles along the route. A man would jump from his horse, grab his mail bags, and be off on a new mount in two minutes. Each man usually rode for about 75 miles before stopping to rest and handing the mail over to another rider. Of course, if the next man could not ride, the first one had to keep going. Altogether there were about 190 stations, 400 station keepers, 400 horses, and 80 riders.

Riders carried the mail in leather pouches, strapped to the saddle. The load for one rider was never over twenty pounds. The postage rate started out at $5 for a half-ounce. That was later changed to $1 for a half-ounce.

The first Pony Express run covered a distance of 1,996 miles in ten days. Later, the same distance was covered in eight or nine days. The best time was made in November of 1860, when news of President Lincoln's election was carried from Ft. Kearny, Nebraska, to Ft. Churchill, Nevada, in six days.

Pony Express mail service ended on October 24, 1861, when the new cross-country telegraph lines were ready for service. The end of the Pony Express meant the ruin of William Russell. His company never made money on the venture, and he was never awarded the government contract he had hoped to win. Still, he did contribute to the pages of history with his daring and exciting enterprise.

2. After students read the information once, they met again in their small groups to discuss the information and rewrite any statements that needed revision or qualification. For example, they corrected the first statement to read "When riding west, Pony Express riders began in St. Joseph, Missouri."

3. To refine and extend comprehension, students worked in groups to write scenes that dramatized some aspect of the text information, elaborating creatively as they wished. Here are descriptions of a few of the Readers' Theater scenes they created and enacted for the class:

- an interview between an aspiring rider and a Pony Express hiring agent
- a conversation between two riders at a rest station
- an interview between a newspaper reporter and a Pony Express rider

4. To engage students in further thinking, the teacher presented the Pony Express as the topic for a Cubing writing activity. She organized students in groups of four, focused all the students on the same kind

of thinking for each round of writing, and had students read aloud what they wrote in their small groups at the end of each round. These were the prompts she used: *describe* a Pony Express rider, *analyze* the workings of the Pony Express, *compare and contrast* the Pony Express with a present-day express-delivery service, *associate* other words and terms with the Pony Express, *argue in favor of or against* the Pony Express, and *apply* something you learned about the Pony Express to some aspect of your own life.

5. The teacher engaged students in a final discussion of what they learned about the Pony Express and then, as a final check on learning, administered a quiz that included multiple choice questions, short-answer questions, and essay questions, each of which involved different levels of thinking.

Sample Lesson #6

Subject: Mathematics

Grade Level: Grade 9

Topic: Circles and Angles

Purposes:

- Orient students to the topic and assess their related knowledge
- Engage students in inferential thinking and hypothesizing so as to strengthen these thinking skills while also piquing their curiosity
- Keep students actively involved in learning through the use of an engaging, thought-provoking activity
- Engage students in collaborative thinking so as to maintain their attention and interest while also allowing them to pool their knowledge and skills

Strategies:

DRTA

Think Pair Share

Read Talk Write

Learning Logs

1. At the beginning of a unit on circles, the teacher organized students into small groups and distributed the exercise on the next page for them to work on collaboratively for about 10 minutes. Students had not been given specific instruction about any of the terms, so they did not know for sure what the correct responses were. Using their general knowledge of vocabulary along with inferential thinking, they formed hypotheses. This was the first step in a DRTA with expository material.

2. Next, groups shared their thinking as a whole class. The teacher facilitated the discussion, aiming for the students to achieve consensus. She provided occasional hints to guide students' thinking to the correct answers but stated the expectation that students would think for themselves and listen to each other instead of waiting for her to

Circles and Angles

DIRECTIONS: Match each term with an illustration. You're not expected to know the correct matches, but use whatever knowledge you have to make educated guesses. Be perpared to share and justify your answers with the other groups.

_____ 1. Tangent

_____ 2. Inscribed circle

_____ 3. Circumscribed circle

_____ 4. Concentric circles

_____ 5. Central angle

_____ 6. Inscribed angle

_____ 7. Minor arc

give them the correct answers. It took another 15 minutes for the groups to work together to match terms and illustrations correctly. The teacher confirmed that they had arrived at the correct answers. Each student was now expected to have the correct matches indicated on his or her own paper.

3. Students worked first in pairs, using only the terms and the illustrative diagrams and a variation of Read Talk Write, to generate tentative definitions. Pairs then teamed up with other pairs to share their thinking and compose an agreed-upon definition, which each student then wrote on his or her own paper. About 15 minutes was allowed for this. No one finished all seven definitions, so completing them became that night's homework. The teacher cautioned students to continue working without looking up the definitions. "I want to see what sense you can make of these terms on your own first. Your thinking and your own words are what count!"

4. For the last 10 minutes of the class, the teacher had students engage in 5 minutes of writing in their Learning Logs to review what they

had done and learned in the lesson and gave them a few minutes of (Think) Pair Share in partners: the students read aloud what they had written to their partners. She collected these writings at the end of the period and later did a quick check of these to assess students' understanding of the concepts so far.

5. The next day, for 10 minutes at the beginning of the period, students shared in small groups the definitions they had generated for homework, again using Think Pair Share. As they were engaged in this, the teacher circulated and checked that each student had completed the homework.

6. Next, students turned to a page in their mathematics textbook that contained definitions of the terms they had been working with. The teacher gave them 15 minutes in their groups to compare their own definitions with the ones in the book and prepare to explain in their own words the definition of each term. (This was a variation on Read Talk Write; students were allowed to keep their books open as they read and discussed, and they composed their final definitions as a group.) One person was to be the reporter for each group.

7. As the reporters gave the definition of the terms, the teacher elaborated as needed and explained any aspects of the textbook definitions that the students didn't understand. This took 15 minutes.

8. Students put away all their books and notes and took out a fresh sheet of paper. The teacher put the terms, matched with the illustrations, on the board and asked students to write the definition of each on their paper. She collected these at the end of the period and used them as another assessment of learning.

Sample Lesson #7

Subject: World History

Grade Level: Grade 10

Topic: Alexander the Great

Purposes:

- Orient students to the topic and assess their related knowledge
- Engage students in hypothesizing and inductive reasoning to strengthen these thinking skills while arousing their curiosity about the topic
- Engage students in collaborative thinking so as to sharpen their critical thinking and make learning enjoyable
- Keep students actively involved in learning through the use of engaging, thought-provoking activities

Strategies:

List Group Label

Carousel

Key Word Notes

Graphic Organizer

1. Before reading the informational selection about Alexander the Great, the teacher organized students into small groups and gave each group a set of cards with the following words on them along with several blank cards. The directions were to put the words into at least two groups (more if desired), label the groups on blank cards, and speculate about the topic (List Group Label).

Macedonia	cooperation	356 B.C.	Achilles	Alexandria
Aristotle	Darius	physical fitness	King Phillip II	Hindu Kush
Egypt	*Iliad*	16	Persia	Babylon
Persian princess	literature and philosophy	military tactics	26	trade

2. After students worked for about 15 minutes on the listing, grouping, and labeling, the teacher stopped the class and had students walk around the room for about 5 minutes, in silence, to examine the categorizing the other small groups had done. Students then returned to their original groups and had another 10 minutes to make any revisions to their arrangements they might want to make and to speculate on the topic.

3. Next, the class as a whole discussed their ideas about the topic, defending their hypotheses by referring to the words in the card set.

4. The teacher then distributed the article for students to read. As they read, they discussed the information in their work groups and made changes in the way they had categorized and labeled the cards.

Alexander the Great

Alexander the Great was born in 356 B.C. in Macedonia, to King Philip II, conqueror of Greece, and Olympias, a Greek woman. Olympias told her son that he was descended directly from Achilles, hero of the Trojan War. This story so inspired Alexander that he carried a copy of Homer's *Iliad* with him until he died.

When he was a boy, Alexander was educated according to the highest Greek standards, which included training in physical fitness and military tactics as well as the study of literature and philosophy. King Philip, wanting only the best for his son, engaged Aristotle as Alexander's tutor. This formal schooling lasted only until Alexander was 16, however, when Philip made Alexander an administrator in his government. Two years later, Philip took Alexander to war with him, putting the young man in charge of the cavalry. The campaign was successful and brought the whole of Greece under Philip's control. Philip planned to conquer the Persians next, but he was killed by one of his own men. Alexander inherited the throne. He was 20 years old.

Alexander was a fierce and dedicated warrior. He expected his father's subjects to accept his rule, and when some of the cities tried to revolt, he treated them harshly. When Thebes tried to break free of Macedonian rule, for instance, Alexander destroyed the city and sold thousands into slavery.

In 334 B.C., after liberating Egypt from Persian rule and establishing the city of Alexandria (which he named after himself), Alexander moved into Asia, intent on conquering the vast Persian Empire. In 331 B.C., after many hardships and battles, he won the Battle of Arbela against Darius, King of the Persians, and Darius fled. This was an unexpected victory because Darius had many more men than did Alexander. Alexander won because he had a better battle plan and his men were better disciplined. He then pursued Darius into the mountains, and when the defeated ruler could not muster troops to fight again, he was killed by his own men. At the age of 26, Alexander was the ruler of a vast territory, having accomplished what his own father had dreamed of.

Many stories of Alexander's prowess have been passed down through history. One of the most popular involves his taming of a great, wild horse, which he named Bucephalus. He was very fond of the horse and rode it all the way to India. When the animal died there, Alexander built a city around its grave and named it Bucephala.

Alexander explored his new empire for several years, traveling across the Hindu Kush, beyond the Indus River, and along the coast of the Arabian Sea. He administered his empire from Babylon, eager to improve trade and cooperation among the peoples he had conquered. To ease relations between the Macedonians and Persians, he married a Persian princess (a daughter of Darius) and performed a ceremony in which thousands of his own men were wed to Persian women.

Alexander dreamed of great things for his empire, but he died before he could accomplish half of what he envisioned. In the spring of 323 B.C., he fell ill with a fever and died in Babylon in the early summer.

5. To help students deepen their comprehension of the material, the teacher next guided them through a rereading of the article, using the Key Word Notes strategy with the three segments of the text as shown

here. Because students had discussed many of the words in the List Group Label activity and had seen those in their first reading, most of them noticed different words and used them in this rereading. Here's one set of notes as an example. This student incorporated information from both readings into her summary

1 tutor administrator cavalry	2 harsh Persia unexpected	3 Bucephala explored fever

Alexander was born in Macedonia. He was the son of a king, and he had a tutor until he was 16 years old. Aristotle was his tutor. Then his father decided he'd had enough school and put him to work. Alexander was a government official first, an administrator, and then he went to war with his father. He was the head of the cavalry. They won, but the king was killed. That's how Alexander got to be king. He was 20 years old.

Alexander was a strong king. He had to be because one of his father's soldiers had killed his father, so some of the people were against him. He kept order by being harsh, like when he destroyed a whole city and turned everyone into slaves because they didn't want him as a king. He won a war against the Persian king, which is what his father had wanted to do. The win was a surprise because the Persian king was very powerful and had a lot more men, but Alexander had a good plan and he won.

Alexander's favorite horse was Bucephala. He named a city in India after the horse when it died. Alexander traveled a lot all over his empire. He wanted people to get along and trade with one another. He had a lot of plans for his empire, but then he died. He died in Babylon. He was born in 356 b.c. and he died in 323 BC, so he was 33 when he died.

6. Finally, students worked in their groups to create an illustrated time line of Alexander's life that they posted in the room. The time-line graphic organizer reinforced the students' understanding of the sequence of events in Alexander's life. Since each group represented the key events in somewhat different ways, seeing the different time lines posted served as additional reinforcement to the learning.

Sample Lesson #8

Subject: Language Arts

Grade Level: Grade 11

Topic: Descriptive Writing

Purposes:

- Develop vocabulary and comprehension skills
- Help students to develop skill with word choice in their writing
- Provide practice with thinking in terms of analogies
- Refine students' descriptive writing abilities
- Motivate students to want to write and share their work

Strategies:

Saturation Reporting

Freewriting

Think Pair Share

Cloze Procedure

Analogies

1. An English teacher gave students their choices of locations on which to base a Saturation Report. They made their observations after school or on the weekend and brought their notes and impressions to class.

2. To help students focus on the locations they had visited in preparation for writing, the teacher had them do a Focused Free-writing for 10 minutes. They wrote without stopping about what they had seen, heard, felt, etc. At the end of the 10 minutes, they paired up, read their freewritings to each other, and talked for a few minutes about the general impression they had of their respective places. This was a variant of Think Pair Share, with the freewriting serving as the thinking time. The writing and talking helped students formulate ideas for their drafts, which they worked on for the rest of the period.

3. The next day, the teacher engaged students in the Cloze Procedure, using a passage written by a professional writer about a memorable location. The teacher had left out a number of the most vivid adjectives and verbs, and students worked in small groups to decide on words that might go in the blanks, using a thesaurus to find the best possible words. Groups then shared their thinking with the whole class, explaining the reasons for their choices. The teacher then handed out the intact passage and students compared the words they had chosen with the ones used by the author.

4. Students returned to their first drafts to improve the adjectives and verbs they had used. They had the choice of working individually or in pairs and were encouraged to use a thesaurus.

5. The next day, the teacher engaged students in work on Analogies that focused on description, showing how the analogies could be the basis of comparisons that would enliven descriptions. For example, the teacher used these two analogies as models, taking care to focus on the nature of the relationship so as to generate effective comparisons:

people : train station :: geese : field

The noise of people talking and jostling each other at the crowded train station reminded me of the clamor of geese honking and nudging each other on the school's soccer field.

woman : restaurant :: queen : court

The elegant woman swept into the restaurant as if she were a queen making an appearance at court.

Students worked in pairs or small groups to generate their own analogies and related descriptions from the information they were using in their Saturation Reports. They incorporated some of these into their reports as they prepared their final copies.

6. Students shared their final reports by compiling them into a booklet and exchanging it with the compiled reports from another class that was engaged in the same assignment.

Bibliography

Aaronson, E., Blaney, N., Stephen, C., Sikes, J., & Snapp, M. (1978). *The jigsaw classroom*. Beverly Hills, CA: Sage.

Abt, C. (1970). *Serious games*. New York: Viking.

Allen, S. (2003). An analytic comparison of three models of reading strategy instruction. *IRAL: International Review of Applied Linguistics in Language Teaching, 41*(4), 319–339.

Allington, R. L. (2001). *What really matters for struggling readers: Designing research-based programs*. New York: Addison Wesley Longman.

Anderson, L. W., Krathwohl, D. R., Airasian, P. W., Cruikshank, K. A., Mayer, R. E., Pintrich, P. R., et al. (Eds.). (2001). *A taxonomy for learning, teaching, and assessing: A revision of Bloom's taxonomy of educational objectives*. New York: Longman.

Angiolino, A. (1995). *Super sharp paper & pencil games*. New York: Sterling.

Applebee, A. (1996). *Curriculum as conversation: Transforming traditions of teaching and learning*. Chicago: University of Chicago Press.

Atwell, N. (Ed.). (1989). *Coming to know: Writing to learn in the intermediate grades*. Portsmouth, NH: Heinemann.

Baird, J., & White, R. (1984, April). *Improving learning through enhanced metacognition: A classroom study*. Paper presented at the 68th meeting of the American Educational Research Association, New Orleans.

Bakunas, B., & Holley, W. (2001). Teaching organization skills. *Clearing House, 74*(3), 151–154.

Barone, D. M., & Morrow, L. M. (Eds.). (2003). *Literacy and young children: Research-based practices*. New York: Guilford Press.

Beers, K. (2002). *When kids can't read: What teachers can do*. Portsmouth, NH: Heinemann.

Belanoff, P., Elbow, P., & Fontaine, S. I. (Eds.). (1991). *Nothing begins with N: New investigations of freewriting*. New York: Oxford University Press.

Bloom, B., Englehart, M., Furst, E., Hill, W., & Krathwohl, D. (1956). *Taxonomy of educational objectives: The classification of educational goals: Handbook I: Cognitive domain*. New York: David McKay.

Bomer, R. (1995). *Time for meaning: Crafting literate lives in middle and high school*. Portsmouth, NH: Heinemann.

Bormuth, J. R. (1962). *Cloze tests as a measure of comprehension ability and readability.* Unpublished doctoral dissertation, Indiana University, Bloomington.

Bormuth, J. R. (1968, April). The cloze readability procedure. *Elementary English, 45,* 429–436.

Bowen, C. (2001). A process approach: The i-search with grade 5—They learn! *Teacher Librarian, 29*(2), 14–18.

Bransford, J. D. (1979). *Human cognition.* Belmont, CA: Wadsworth.

Britton, J. (1970). *Language and learning.* London: Penguin.

Britton, J. (1979). *A reader's expectations.* In G. Pradl (Ed.), *Prospect and retrospect: Selected essays of James Britton* (pp. 130–138). London: Heinemann.

Britton, J., Burgess, T., Martin, N., McLeod, A., & Rosen, H. (1975). *The development of writing abilities 11–18.* London: Macmillan.

Bromley, K., Modlo, M., & Irwin-De Vitis, L. (1995). *Graphic organizers: Visual strategies for active learning.* New York: Scholastic.

Brown, A. L., & Campione, J. C. (1992). Students as researchers and teachers. In J. W. Keefe & H. J. Walberg (Eds.), *Teaching for thinking* (pp. 49–57). Reston, VA: National Association of Secondary School Principals.

Brown, A. L., Palincsar, A. S., & Purcell, L. (1986). Poor readers: Teach, don't label. In U. Neisser (Ed.), *The school achievement of minority children: New perspectives* (pp. 105–143). Hillsdale, NJ: Lawrence Erlbaum Associates.

Brozo, W. G., & Simpson, M. L. (1999). *Readers, teachers, learners: Expanding literacy across the content areas.* Upper Saddle River, NJ: Merrill.

Bruner, J. (1960). *The process of education.* Cambridge, MA: Harvard University Press.

Bruner, J. (1973). *Going beyond the information given.* New York: Norton.

Bruner, J., Goodnow, J., & Austin, A. (1956). *A study of thinking.* New York: Wiley.

Buehl, D. (2001). *Classroom strategies for interactive learning.* Newark, DE: International Reading Association.

Butler, P. (2002). Imitation as freedom: (Re)forming student writing. *The Quarterly, 24*(2), 25–32. Berkeley, CA: National Writing Project.

Buzan, T., & Buzan, B. (1993). *The mind map book: How to use radiant thinking to maximize your brain's untapped potential.* New York: Penguin.

Carr, E., Dewitz, P., & Patberg, J. (1989). Using cloze for inference training with expository text. *The Reading Teacher 43*(6), 380–385.

Carr, E., & Ogle, D. M. (1987). K-W-L-Plus: A strategy for comprehension and summarization. *Journal of Reading, 30*(7), 626–631.

Clarkson, A., & Cross, G. B. (1984). *World folktales.* New York: Scribner.

Cooper, E. J. (2004). The pursuit of equity and excellence in educational opportunity. In D. Lapp, C. C. Block, E. J. Cooper, J. Flood, N. Roser, & J. V. Tinajero (Eds.), *Teaching all the children: Strategies for developing literacy in an urban setting* (pp. 12–30). New York: Guilford Press.

Cornelius, M., & Parr, A. (1991). *What's your game? A resource book for mathematical activities.* Cambridge: Cambridge University Press.

Cowan, G., & Cowan, E. (1980). *Writing.* New York: Wiley.

Cunningham, P. M., Hall, D. P., & Cunningham, J. W. (2000). *Guided reading the four-blocks way.* Greensboro, NC: Carson-Dellosa.

Dahl, K. L., & Farnan, N. (1998). *Children's writing: Perspectives from research.* Newark, DE: International Reading Association.

Davidson, J., & Wilkerson, B. (1988). *Directed reading-thinking activities.* Monroe, NY: Trillium Press.

Decker-Collins, N. L. (1990). Freewriting, personal writing, and the at-risk reader. *Journal of Reading, 33*(8), 654–655.

Dixon, C. N., & Nessel, D. D. (1983). *Language-experience approach to reading (and writing): LEA for ESL.* Hayward, CA: Alemany Press.

Dixon, C. N., & Nessel, D. D. (1992). *Meaning making: Directed reading and thinking activities for second-language students.* Englewood Cliffs, NJ: Alemany Press.

Dougherty-Stahl, K. A. (2004). Proof, practice, and promise: Comprehension strategy instruction in the primary grades. *The Reading Teacher, 57*(7), 598–609.

Duke, C. (1981). Saturation writing. *The Quarterly, 4*(1). Retrieved February 20, 2006, from http://www.writingproject.org/cs/nwpp/print/nwpr/1848

Duke, N., & Bennett-Armistead, V. S. (2003). *Reading and writing information text in the primary grades.* New York: Scholastic.

Dunston, P. J. (1992). A critique of graphic organizer research. *Reading Research and Instruction, 31*(2), 57–65.

Elbow, P. (1973). *Writing without teachers.* New York: Oxford University Press.

Elbow, P. (1981). *Writing with power.* New York: Oxford University Press.

Emig, J. (1977). Writing as a mode of learning. *College Composition and Communication, 28*(2), 122–127.

Fader, D., & Shaevitz, M. (1966). *Hooked on books.* New York: Berkley.

Frayer, D., Frederick, W. C., & Klausmeier, H. J. (1969). *A schema for testing the level of cognitive mastery.* Madison, WI: Wisconsin Center for Education Research.

Fulweiler, T. (1980). Journals across the disciplines. *English Journal, 69*(12), 14–19.

Geeslin, W. E. (1977). Using writing about mathematics as a teaching technique. *Mathematics Teacher, 70*(5), 112–115.

Goodman, K. (1967, May). Reading: A psycholinguistic guessing game. *Journal of the Reading Specialist, 6,* 126–135.

Greene, S. (1991). *Mining texts in reading to write* (Occasional Paper No. 29). Berkeley, CA: National Writing Project.

Hammond, W. D. (1984). *Reading comprehension: Make every child a winner.* A Learning Institute Coursebook. Belmont, CA: Learning Institute.

Heath, B. (1994, Fall). Scrambled sentences: A puzzle worth solving. *The Law Teacher* (a publication of the Gonzaga University School of Law).

Herber, H. (1978). *Teaching reading in the content areas.* Englewood Cliffs, NJ: Prentice Hall.

Hillebrand, R. (2004). Beyond primer prose: Two ways to imitate the masters. *The Quarterly, 26*(2), 34–36. Berkeley, CA: National Writing Project.

Hubalek, L. K. (1995). *A trail of thread: A woman's westward journey.* Aurora, CO: Butterfield.

Huff-Benkoski, K. A., & Greenwood, S. C. (1995). The use of word analogy instruction with developing readers. *The Reading Teacher, 48*(5), 446–447.

Hyerle, D. (1996). *Visual tools for constructing knowledge.* Alexandria, VA: Association for Supervision and Curriculum Development.

Hyerle, D. (2000). *A field guide to visual tools.* Alexandria, VA: Association for Supervision and Curriculum Development.

Jackson, Y. (2005). Unlocking the potential of African-American students: Keys to reversing underachievement. *Theory Into Practice, 44*(3), 203–210.

Jensen, E. (1998). *Teaching with the brain in mind.* Alexandria, VA: Association for Supervision and Curriculum Development.

Jensen, E. (2005). *Teaching with the brain in mind* (2nd ed.). Alexandria, VA: Association for Supervision and Curriculum Development.

Johnson, D. W., Johnson, R. T., & Holubec, E. (1998). *Cooperation in the classroom.* Boston: Allyn & Bacon.

Joyce, B., Weil, M., & Calhoun, E. (2000). *Models of teaching* (6th ed.). Boston: Allyn & Bacon.

Kagan, S. (1994). *Cooperative learning.* San Clemente, CA: Resources for Teachers.

Keene, E. O., & Zimmerman, S. (1997). *Mosaic of thought: Teaching comprehension in a reader's workshop.* Portsmouth, NH: Heinemann.

Kelley, E. C. (1947). *Education for what is real.* New York: Harper & Brothers.

Ketch, A. (2005). Conversation: The comprehension connection. *The Reading Teacher, 59*(1), 8–13.

Klausmeier, H. J., Ghatala, E., & Frayer, D. A. (1974). *Conceptual learning and development: A cognitive view.* New York: Academic Press.

Knapp, M. S. (1995). *Teaching for meaning in high-poverty classrooms.* New York: Teachers College Press.

Langer, J. (2002). *Effective literacy instruction: Building successful reading and writing programs.* Urbana, IL: National Council of Teachers of English.

Lengling, M. (1995, March). *The use of readers' theater in the ELF classroom.* Paper presented at the Meeting of the Teacher of English to Speakers of Other Languages, Long Beach, CA.

Lenski, S., & Ehlers-Zavala, F. (2004). *Reading strategies for Spanish speakers.* Dubuque, IA: Kendall/Hunt.

Lenski, S. D., Wham, M. A., & Johns, J. L. (1999). *Reading and learning strategies for middle and high school students.* Dubuque, IA: Kendall/Hunt.

Lewis, M., & Wray, D., (1995). *Developing children's non-fiction writing.* Leamington Spa, England: Scholastic.

Lewis, M., Wray, D., & Rospigliosi, P. (1994). ". . . and I want it in your own words." *The Reading Teacher, 47*(7), 528–536.

Lyman, F. (1981). *The responsive classroom discussion.* In A. S. Anderson (Ed.), *Mainstreaming digest* (pp. 109–113). College Park, MD: University of Maryland College of Education.

Lysynchuk, L. M., Pressley, M., & Vye, N. J. (1990). Reciprocal teaching improves standardized reading-comprehension performance in poor comprehenders. *The Elementary School Journal, 90*(5), 469–484.

Macrorie, K. (1976). *Searching writing: Making knowledge personal.* Rochelle Park, NJ: Hayden.

Macrorie, K. (1988). *The i-search paper: Revised edition of searching writing.* Portsmouth, NH: Boynton/Cook.

Mahiri, J. (1998). *Shooting for excellence: African American youth and culture in new century schools.* Urbana, IL: National Council of Teachers of English.

Mahiri, J. (2004). *What they don't learn in school: Literacy in the lives of urban youth.* New York: Peter Lang.

Marzano, R. J., Pickering, D. J., Arredondo, D. E., Blackburn, G. J., Brandt, R. S., & Moffett, C. A. (1992). *Dimensions of learning: An integrative instructional framework.* Alexandria, VA: Association for Supervision and Curriculum Development and Mid-continent Regional Educational Laboratory.

Marzano, R. J., Pickering, D. J., & Pollock, J. E. (2001). *Classroom instruction that works: Research-based strategies for student achievement.* Alexandria, VA: Association for Supervision and Curriculum Development.

McTighe, J., & Lyman, F. T. (1988). Cueing thinking in the classroom: The promise of theory-embedded tools. *Educational Leadership, 45*(7), 18–24.

Moffett, J. (1968). *A student-centered language arts curriculum K-13.* Boston: Houghton Mifflin.

Moffett, J. (1973). *A student-centered language arts curriculum K-13* (1973 impression). Boston: Houghton Mifflin.

Moffett, J. (1992). *Active voice: A writing program across the curriculum.* Montclair, NJ: Boynton/Cook.

Moore, D., Bean, T., Birdyshaw, D., & Rycik, J. (1999). *Adolescent literacy: A position statement.* Newark, DE: International Reading Association.

Moore, D. W., & Moore, S. A. (1986). Possible sentences. In E. K. Dishner, T. W. Bean, J. E. Readence, & D. W. Moore (Eds.), *Reading in the content areas: Improving classroom instruction* (2nd ed., pp. 174–179). Dubuque, IA: Kendall/Hunt.

Moore, D. W., & Moore, S. A. (1992). Possible sentences: An update. In E. K. Dishner, T. W. Bean, J. E. Readence, & D. W. Moore (Eds.), *Reading in the content areas: Improving classroom instruction* (3rd ed., pp. 196–202). Dubuque, IA: Kendall/Hunt.

Moore, D., & Readance, J. (1984). A meta-analysis of the effect of graphic organizers on learning from text. *Journal of Educational Research, 78*(1), 11–17.

Moses, R. P., & Cobb, C. E., Jr. (2001). *Radical equations: Math literacy and civil rights.* Boston: Beacon Press.

National Council of Teachers of English. (2004). *A call to action: What we know about adolescent literacy and ways to support teachers in meeting students' needs* (A Position/Action Statement from NCTE's Commission on Reading). Urbana, IL: National Council of Teachers of English.

National Institute of Child Health and Human Development. (2000). *The report of the national reading panel: Teaching children to read: An evidence-based assessment of the scientific research literature on reading and its implications for reading instruction* (NIH Publication No. 00–47699). Washington, DC: Author.

Nelson-Herber, J. (1985). Anticipation and prediction in reading comprehension. In T. L. Harris & E. J. Cooper (Eds.), *Reading, thinking, and concept development: Strategies for the classroom* (pp. 89–103). New York: College Entrance Examination Board.

Nessel, D. (1987). Reading comprehension: Asking the right questions. *Phi Delta Kappan, 68*(6), 442–444.

Nessel, D., & Jones, M. (1981). *The language-experience approach to reading: A handbook for teachers.* New York: Teachers College Press.

Nessel, D., Jones, M., & Dixon, C. (1989). *Thinking through the language arts.* New York: Macmillan.

Nessel, D., & Newbold, F. (2003). *180 think-aloud math word problems.* New York: Scholastic.

Nichols, J. (1980). Using paragraph frames to help remedial high school students with written assignments. *Journal of Reading, 24,* 228–231.

Norwood, K. S., & Carter, G. (1996). Journal writing: An insight into students' understanding. In D. V. Lambdin, P. E. Kehle, & R. V. Preston (Eds.), *Emphasis on assessment: Readings from NCTM's school-based journals.* Reston, VA: National Council of Teachers of Mathematics.

Nystrand, M., Gamoran, A., Kachur, R., & Prendergast, C. (1997). *Opening dialogue: Understanding the dynamics of language and learning in the English classroom.* New York: Teachers College Press.

Ogle, D. (1986a). K-W-L: A teaching model that develops active reading of expository text. *The Reading Teacher, 39*(6), 564–570.

Ogle, D. (1986b). K-W-L group instructional strategy. In A. Palincsar, D. Ogle, B. Jones, & E. Carr (Eds.), *Teaching reading as thinking* (Teleconference Resource Guide, pp. 11–17). Alexandria, VA: Association for Supervision and Curriculum Development.

Palincsar, A. S., & Brown, A. (1984). Reciprocal teaching of comprehension-fostering and comprehension monitoring activities. *Cognition and Instruction, 1*(2), 117–175.

Palincsar, A. S., & Brown, A. L. (1985). Reciprocal teaching: Activities to promote "reading with your mind." In T. L. Harris & E. J. Cooper (Eds.), *Reading, thinking, and concept development: Strategies for the classroom* (pp. 147–158). New York: The College Entrance Examination Board.

Palincsar, A. S., & Brown, A. L. (1986). Interactive teaching to promote independent learning from text. *The Reading Teacher, 39*(8), 771–777.

Palincsar, A. S., & Klenk, L. J. (1991). Dialogues promoting reading comprehension. In B. Means, C. Chelemer, & M. S. Knapp (Eds.), *Teaching advanced skills to at-risk students* (pp. 112–140). San Francisco: Jossey-Bass.

Palincsar, A. S., & Klenk, L. (1992). Fostering literacy learning in supportive contexts. *Journal of Learning Disabilities, 25*(4), 211–225, 229.

Pauk, W. (1974). *How to study in college.* Boston: Houghton Mifflin.

Paul, R. (1995). *Critical thinking: How to prepare students for a rapidly changing world.* Dillon Beach, CA: Foundation for Critical Thinking.

Paul, R., & Elder, L. (2005). *Learn the tools the best thinkers use.* Upper Saddle River, NJ: Prentice Hall.

Paznik-Bondarin, J., & Baxter, M. (1987). *Write and write again.* New York: Macmillan.

Pikulski, J. J., & Tobin, A. W. (1982). The Cloze Procedure as an informal assessment technique. In J. J. Pikulski & T. Shanahan (Eds.), *Approaches to the informal evaluation of reading* (pp. 42–62). Newark, DE: International Reading Association.

Pogrow, S. A. (1990). Challenging at-risk students: Findings from the HOTS program. *Phi Delta Kappan, 71*(5), 389–397.

Pogrow, S. (2000, April 19). Beyond the "good start" mentality: Overcoming the cognitive wall for disadvantaged students in grades 4–8. *Education Week,* pp. 44–46.

Pohl, M. (2000). *Learning to think, thinking to learn: Models and strategies to develop a classroom culture of thinking.* Cheltenham, Australia: Hawker Brownlow.

Polya, G. (1945). *How to solve it: A new aspect of mathematical method.* Princeton: Princeton University Press.

Postman, N., & Weingartner, C. (1969). *Teaching as a subversive activity.* New York; Dell.

Rasinski, T. (2000). Speed does matter in reading. *Reading Teacher, 54*(2), 146–151.

Read, S. (2001). Kid mice hunt for their selfs: First and second graders writing research. *Language Arts, 78*(4), 333–342.

Rester-Zodrow, G., & Chancer, J. (1997). *Moon journals: Writing, art, and inquiry through focused nature study.* Portsmouth, NH: Heinemann.

Robb, L. (2003). *Teaching reading in social studies, science, and math.* New York: Scholastic.

Robinson, A. (1993). *What smart students know.* New York: Crown.

Rose, M. (1989). *Lives on the boundary.* New York: Penguin.

Rothstein, E., & Lauber, G. (2000). *Writing as learning: A content-based approach.* Thousand Oaks, CA: Corwin Press.

Shafer, G. (1999). Re-envisioning research. *English Journal, 89*(1), 45–50.

Singham, M. (1998). The canary in the mine: The achievement gap between black and white students. *Phi Delta Kappan, 80*(1), 9–15.

Smith, M., & Wilhelm, J. (2002). *Reading don't fix no Chevys: Literacy in the lives of young men.* Portsmouth, NH: Heinemann.

Solomon, E. (1993). *Games with paper and pencil.* New York: Dover.

Stahl, N. A., King, J. R., & Henk, W. A. (1991). Enhancing students' notetaking through training and evaluation. *Journal of Reading, 34*(8), 614–622.

Stahl, R. J. (1990). *Using "think-time" behaviors to promote students' information processing, learning, and on-task participation. An instructional module.* Tempe, AZ: Arizona State University.

Stahl, S. A., & Kapinus, B. A. (1991). Possible sentences: Predicting word meanings to teach content area vocabulary. *The Reading Teacher, 45*(1), 36–43.

Stauffer, R. G. (1969). *Teaching reading as a thinking process.* New York: Harper & Row.

Stauffer, R. G. (1975). *Directing the reading-thinking process.* New York: Harper & Row.

Stauffer, R. G., Burrows, A. T., & Horn, T. D. (1960). *The Winston basic readers.* New York: Holt, Rinehart & Winston.

Strong, W. J. (2005). *Write for insight: Empowering content learning, grades 6–12.* Boston: Allyn & Bacon.

Taba, H. (1967). *A teacher's handbook to elementary social studies.* Palo Alto, CA: Addison-Wesley.

Taba, H., Durkin, M. C., Fraenkel, J. R., & NcNaughton, A. H. (1971). *A teacher's handbook to elementary social studies: An inductive approach* (2nd ed.). Reading, MA: Addison-Wesley.

Taylor, B. M., Pressley, M., & Pearson, P. D. (2002). Research-supported characteristics of teachers and schools that promote reading achievement. In B. M. Taylor & P. D. Pearson (Eds.), *Teaching reading: Effective schools, accomplished teachers* (pp. 361–373). Mahwah, NJ: Erlbaum.

Taylor, W. (1953). Cloze Procedure: A new tool for measuring readability. *Journalism Quarterly, 30*(4), 415–433.

Tierney, R. J., & Readence, J. E. (2005). *Reading strategies and practices: A compendium* (6th ed.). Boston: Allyn & Bacon.

Tomlinson, C. (2001). *How to differentiate instruction in mixed ability classrooms.* Alexandria, VA: Association for Supervision and Curriculum Development.

Torbe, M., & Medway, P. (1981). *The climate for learning.* Montclair, NJ: Boynton/Cook.

Vacca, R. T., & Vacca, J. L. (2002). *Content area reading: Literacy and learning across the curriculum.* Boston: Allyn & Bacon.

van Garderen, D. (2004). Reciprocal teaching as a comprehension strategy for understanding mathematical word problems. *Reading & Writing Quarterly, 20*(2), 225–229.

Vaughan, J., & Estes, T. (1986). *Reading and reasoning beyond the primary grades.* Boston: Allyn & Bacon.

Venville, G. & Dawson, V. (2004). *The art of teaching science.* Sydney, Australia: Allen and Unwin.

Vygotsky, L. S. (1962). *Thought and language.* E. Hanfmann & G. Vakar (Eds. and Trans.). Cambridge, MA: MIT Press. (Original work published 1934)

Vygotsky, L. S. (1978). *Mind and society: The development of higher mental processes.* Cambridge, MA: Harvard University Press. (Original work published 1930)

Wachsberger, K. (2005). *Transforming lives: A socially responsible guide to the magic of writing and researching.* Ann Arbor, MI: Azenphony Press.

Williams, F. E. (1970). *Classroom ideas for encouraging thinking and feeling.* Buffalo, NY: D.O.K. Publishers.

Williams, F. E. (1993). The cognitive-affective interaction model for enriching gifted programs. In J. S. Renzulli (Ed.), *Systems and models for developing programs for the gifted and talented* (pp. 461–484). Highett, Australia: Hawker Brownlow Education.

Wilson, H. A., & Castner, F. L. (1999). From Mickey Mouse to Marilyn Manson: A search experience. *English Journal, 89*(1), 74–81.

Wolf, J. (2004). *Journal activities that sharpen students' writing: Standards-based activities that spark great ideas, strengthen grammar skills, build writing stamina, and give students practice with all kinds of writing.* New York: Scholastic.

Woods, K., & Harmon, J. M. (2001). *Strategies for integrating reading and writing in middle and high school classrooms.* Westerville, OH: National Middle School Association.

Yopp, R. H., & Yopp, H. K. (1996). *Literature-based reading activities.* Boston: Allyn & Bacon.

Young, T., & Vardell, S. (1993). Weaving readers' theater and nonfiction in the curriculum. *The Reading Teacher, 46*(5), 396–406.

Zainuddin, H., Yahya, N., Morales-Jones, C., & Ariza, J. (2002). *Fundamentals of teaching English to speakers of other languages in K–12 mainstream classrooms.* Dubuque, IA: Kendall/Hunt.

Index

**CORWIN
PRESS**

The Corwin Press logo—a raven striding across an open book—represents the union of courage and learning. Corwin Press is committed to improving education for all learners by publishing books and other professional development resources for those serving the field of PreK–12 education. By providing practical, hands-on materials, Corwin Press continues to carry out the promise of its motto: **"Helping Educators Do Their Work Better."**

DATE DUE

NOV 0 4 REC'D			
APR 2 7 2010			
MAY 0 5 REC'D JUN 0 7 2011			
AUG 2 6 2013			
MAR 2 1 2016			
GAYLORD			PRINTED IN U.S.A.

Other Books From Corwin Press:

ISBN: 1-4129-1384-5

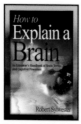

ISBN: 1-4129-0639-3

ISBN: 1-4129-0474-9

Use these strategies to develop your students' thinking skills and increase their learning in all subject areas.

How can teachers improve students' higher-level and creative thinking? The revised edition of this handbook provides strategies and sample lesson plans to help students learn to think more effectively and to raise their achievement levels.

Drawing upon past and recent research, the authors discuss the importance of actively engaging all students—including those with a history of low achievement—in higher levels of thinking. Thirty specific strategies, including K-W-L, Read and Think Math, and Reciprocal Teaching, can be readily integrated into daily lesson plans.

This step-by-step guide shows teachers how to

- Help students develop, refine, and extend their thinking capacities
- Challenge students to creatively approach complex and unfamiliar material
- Encourage students to bring their own perspective to class assignments
- Provide students at all learning levels with appropriate support

With its practical, user-friendly approach, this important resource should be in the hands of every educator!

CORWIN PRESS
A SAGE Publications Company
2455 Teller Road
Thousand Oaks, CA 91320-2218

Call: 800-818-7243 Fax: 800-417-2466
CorwinPress.com

ISBN 1-4129-3881-3

9 781412 938815

90000>